Kitchen Solutions

Substitutions, Basic Formulas and Essential References

Edited by
Jennifer L. Newens

BRISTOL PUBLISHING ENTERPRISES
San Leandro, California

Printed in Hong Kong.

ISBN 1-55867-213-3

Design: Frank J. Paredes
Illustrations: Shanti Nelson
Compiler: Meredith Kornfeld

CONTENTS

While there's no substitute for the real thing, sometimes you must, for one reason or another, make adjustments to recipes. For example:

- You don't have an ingredient in the pantry and can't get to the market to purchase it.

- You need a stand-in for a hard-to-find ingredient.

- You have something that needs to be used before it spoils.

- You want a different variation of a common recipe.

This section is designed to address any of these issues. Use it as a guide when a substitution must be made. Note that some ingredients and their substitutions need different measurements to achieve the same result.

TIP: Use the blank page at the back of the section to record your own substitutions.

If You Don't Have	Use
abalone	clams OR squid (calamari)
aioli	see page 39
almond paste	see page 39
anchovies	anchovy paste OR sardines OR kippers
anchovy paste	anchovies *Crush in a small bowl with a fork.*
anise seeds	fennel seeds OR fresh or dried tarragon
apples, fresh or dried	fresh or dried pears
apple pie spice	see page 39
applejack	Calvados OR armagnac OR apple juice concentrate
apricots, fresh or dried	fresh or dried peaches
arugula	watercress OR peppercress
arrowroot *for thickening* 1 tbs.	1 tbs. cornstarch OR 1 tbs. potato flour (potato starch) OR 2½ tbs. flour
bacon	pancetta OR ham OR Canadian bacon
bacon, Canadian	ham OR cooked bacon
baking powder, double-acting 1 tsp.	½ tsp. baking soda + ½ tsp. cream of tartar OR ¼ tsp. baking soda + ½ cup buttermilk or sour milk, page 17 *Reduce liquid in recipe by ½ cup.*

If You Don't Have	Use
bananas, green *for cooking*	plantains
beans, black	pinto beans OR red beans OR pink beans
beans, butter	lima beans OR fava beans
beans, cranberry	kidney beans OR pinto beans OR pink beans OR red beans
beans, fava	baby lima beans
beans, great Northern	marrow beans OR navy beans
beans, haricot vert	regular green beans, cut lengthwise into slivers
beans, kidney	pinto beans OR red beans OR pink beans OR cranberry beans
beans, lima	fava beans OR butter beans
beans, marrow	great Northern beans
beans, navy	pea beans OR great Northern beans
beans, pea	navy beans
beans, pink	pinto beans OR red beans OR kidney beans OR cranberry beans
beans, pinto	kidney beans OR red beans OR pink beans OR cranberry beans

If You Don't Have	Use
beans, red	pinto beans OR pink beans OR kidney beans OR cranberry beans
beet greens	spinach OR Swiss chard leaves OR turnip greens
berries, blackberries	black or red raspberries OR boysenberries
berries, blueberries	huckleberries
berries, boysenberries	blackberries OR black or red raspberries
berries, huckleberries	blueberries
berries, raspberries	blackberries OR boysenberries OR strawberries
beurre manie	see page 39
biscuit mix	see page 39
blackening spices	see page 40
bok choy	Napa cabbage OR green cabbage
bouquet garni	see page 40
bourbon	blended whiskey
breadcrumbs, dry 1 cup	¾ cup cracker crumbs OR 1 cup wheat germ OR 1 cup fresh breadcrumbs, sautéed *Sauté in a skillet with a small amount of butter until golden brown.* OR 1 cup oatmeal, as a binder
breadcrumbs, fresh 1 cup	3 slices white bread *Process with a blender or food processor to fine crumbs.*
brandy	cognac

If You Don't Have	Use
bread, sandwich	flour tortillas
	OR pita bread
	OR focaccia, split horizontally
broccoli	cauliflower
	OR Brussels sprouts
	OR cabbage
broth, chicken or beef	see stock
Brussels sprouts	cabbage
	OR broccoli
buffalo	beef
	OR venison
bulgur wheat	rice
	OR quinoa
	OR couscous
	OR orzo
butter 1 cup	1 cup margarine
	OR 1 cup vegetable shortening
	OR $\frac{7}{8}$ cup lard
	OR 1 cup applesauce, for baking
	OR 1 cup orange or apple juice concentrate, for baking
butter, clarified	vegetable or canola oil
	OR see page 40
butter, maitre d'hotel	see page 40
buttermilk *for cooking*	plain yogurt
	OR sour milk, see page 17
	OR thinned sour cream
cabbage, green	bok choy
	OR Brussels sprouts
	OR Napa cabbage
	OR Bibb lettuce, for wrappers
Cajun spice blend	see page 40

If You Don't Have	Use
cake, angel food	ladyfingers OR sponge cake OR pound cake
cake, pound	sponge cake OR angel food cake OR ladyfingers
cake, sponge	pound cake OR angel food cake OR ladyfingers
Calvados	applejack OR armagnac OR apple juice concentrate
capers	chopped full-flavored green olives
caraway seeds	dill seeds
cardoons	artichoke hearts
carrots, cooked	cooked parsnips
celery root (celeriac)	celery
champagne	dry white wine OR sparkling grape juice
chard, Swiss *for cooking*	spinach OR beet greens OR kale OR turnip greens
chayote (mirliton)	yellow crookneck squash OR zucchini OR pattypan squash
cheese, Asiago	Parmesan cheese OR dry Jack cheese OR Romano cheese OR other hard grating cheese
cheese, blue	Roquefort cheese OR Stilton cheese OR Gorgonzola cheese
cheese, Brie	Camembert cheese

If You Don't Have	Use
cheese, Camembert	Brie cheese
cheese, chèvre	goat's or sheep's milk feta cheese
cheese, cottage	ricotta cheese OR cream cheese OR yogurt cheese, page 41
cheese, cream	yogurt cheese, page 41 OR pureed ricotta cheese, drained if desired OR pureed cottage cheese, drained if desired OR neufchatel cheese OR mascarpone cheese
cheese, Edam	Gouda cheese
cheese, Emmentaller	Gruyère cheese OR Swiss cheese OR Jarlsberg cheese
cheese, farmer's	cow's milk feta cheese OR queso fresco OR fresh mozzarella cheese
cheese, feta *cow's milk*	queso fresco OR farmer's cheese OR fresh mozzarella cheese
cheese, feta *goat's or sheep's milk*	chèvre
cheese, Gorgonzola	Stilton cheese OR Roquefort cheese OR other blue-veined cheese
cheese, Gouda	Edam cheese
cheese, Gruyère	Swiss cheese OR Jarlsberg cheese OR Emmentaller cheese
cheese, dry Jack	Parmesan cheese OR Asiago cheese OR Romano cheese OR other hard grating cheese

If You Don't Have	Use
cheese, Jarlsberg	Gruyère cheese OR Swiss cheese OR Emmentaller cheese
cheese, mascarpone	cream cheese (do not use low-fat)
cheese, Parmesan	Romano cheese OR dry Jack cheese OR Asiago cheese OR other hard grating cheese
cheese, queso fresco	cow's milk feta cheese OR farmer's cheese OR fresh mozzarella cheese
cheese, ricotta	puréed cottage cheese OR cream cheese OR yogurt cheese, page 41
cheese, Romano	Parmesan cheese OR dry Jack cheese OR Asiago cheese OR other hard grating cheese
cheese, Roquefort	Stilton cheese OR Gorgonzola cheese OR other blue-veined cheese
cheese, Swiss	Gruyère cheese OR Jarlsberg cheese OR Emmentaller cheese
cheese, Stilton	Gorgonzola cheese OR Roquefort cheese OR other blue-veined cheese
cheese, yogurt	cream cheese OR pureed ricotta cheese, drained if desired OR pureed cottage cheese, drained if desired
cherries, dried	dried cranberries OR dried currants OR raisins
chervil, fresh or dried	fresh or dried parsley
chicory	curly endive

If You Don't Have	Use
chili powder	see page 41
chili sauce	see page 41
chives, fresh 1 tbs. chopped	1 tbs. chopped green onion tops
chocolate chips, semisweet 6 oz.	6 oz. semisweet chocolate, chopped
chocolate, milk *for melting* 3 oz.	2¾ oz. semisweet chocolate, chopped + 1 oz. whole milk powder + 1⅓ cups sugar *Heat ingredients in a double boiler over simmering water or in a saucepan over very low heat. Stir until melted and smooth. Take care not to burn mixture.*
chocolate, semisweet *for melting* 1 oz.	3 tbs. unsweetened cocoa powder + 1 tbs. butter, vegetable oil or margarine + 3 tbs. sugar *Mix ingredients together.* OR 1 oz. unsweetened chocolate, chopped + 4 tsp. sugar *Heat ingredients in a double boiler over simmering water or in a saucepan over very low heat. Stir until melted and smooth. Take care not to burn mixture.*
chocolate, unsweetened *for melting* 1 oz.	3 tbs. unsweetened cocoa powder + 1 tbs. butter, vegetable oil or margarine *Heat ingredients in a double boiler over simmering water or in a saucepan over very low heat. Stir until melted and smooth. Take care not to burn mixture.*
cinnamon sugar	see page 41
clams	mussels OR small oysters
cocoa mix, hot	see page 41
coconut cream	1 part grated unsweetened coconut + 1 part hot milk or heavy cream *Process ingredients with a blender or food processor until well blended. Strain mixture, squeezing out as much liquid as possible; discard solids.*

If You Don't Have	Use
coconut milk	1 part grated unsweetened coconut + 1 part very hot water *Process ingredients with a blender or food processor until well blended. Strain mixture, squeezing out as much liquid as possible; discard solids.* OR see page 32
cognac	brandy
Cointreau	Grand Marnier OR Curaçao OR Triple Sec OR orange juice concentrate
collard greens *for cooking*	spinach OR kale OR beet greens OR turnip greens OR mustard greens
corn syrup, light 1 cup	$1\frac{1}{4}$ cups sugar + $\frac{1}{3}$ cup water *Boil until syrupy.*
cornmeal	polenta
cornstarch *for thickening* 1 tbs.	1 tbs. arrowroot OR 1 tbs. potato flour (potato starch) OR $2\frac{1}{2}$ tbs. flour
coulis, fruit or vegetable	see page 41
court-bouillon	see page 42
cranberries, dried	dried cherries OR raisins OR dried currants
couscous	rice OR bulgur wheat OR quinoa
crab	lobster OR shrimp OR crayfish
crab boil	see page 42

If You Don't Have	Use
crayfish (crawfish)	shrimp OR lobster OR crab
cream cheese	see cheese
cream, half-and-half 1 cup	½ cup heavy cream + ½ cup whole milk OR ½ cup evaporated milk + ½ cup milk
cream, heavy *not for whipping* 1 cup	¾ cup whole milk + ⅓ cup butter, melted OR 1 cup evaporated milk
cream, light *for cooking* 1 cup	¾ cup milk + 3 tbs. butter, melted
cream, sour	plain yogurt, drained if desired OR sour milk, page 17 OR crème fraiche, page 42
crème anglaise	see sauce, custard
crème chantilly	see page 42
crème fraiche	¾ cup sour cream + ¼ cup milk, plain yogurt or water OR see page 42
Creole seasoning	see page 43
crepes	thin pancakes OR thin omelets OR hydrated rice paper *Follow instructions on package to hydrate.*
currants, dried	raisins OR chopped dried cherries OR chopped dried cranberries
curry powder	see page 43

If You Don't Have	Use
Curaçao	Grand Marnier OR Cointreau OR Triple Sec OR orange juice concentrate
custard, for baking	see page 43
daikon radish	radishes OR small, tender turnips
dandelion greens *for cooking*	mustard greens
dates, dried	raisins OR dried figs OR prunes
dill seeds	caraway seeds OR dill weed
dressing	see salad dressing
dry rubs	see pages 43-44
duck	goose OR other game bird
egg, whole *for baking* 1	¼ cup egg substitute OR 2 egg yolks + 1 tbs. water OR 2 egg whites OR ¼ cup applesauce
egg yolks *for thickening* 2	1 egg
eggplant	zucchini
endive, Belgian	radicchio
endive, curly *for salads*	chicory OR escarole OR frisee

If You Don't Have	Use
escarole *for salads*	chicory OR curly endive OR frisee
espresso, brewed 1 cup	1 cup drip coffee, brewed double-strength
fennel seeds	anise seeds OR dried tarragon
figs, dried	raisins OR dates OR prunes
fines herbes	see page 44
fish, bluefish	mackerel OR trout OR other tender, strongly flavored fish
fish, grouper	sea bass OR red snapper OR rock cod OR cod OR halibut OR other firm, mild-flavored fish
fish, halibut	cod OR rock cod OR red snapper OR grouper OR sea bass OR other firm, mild-flavored fish
fish, mackerel	bluefish OR trout OR other tender, strongly flavored fish
fish, mako shark	tuna OR swordfish OR other firm, meaty fish
fish, monkfish	lobster
fish, orange roughy	sole OR flounder OR other delicate, flaky fish

If You Don't Have	Use
fish, salmon	trout
	OR tuna
	OR other firm or distinctively flavored fish
fish, sea bass	red snapper
	OR rock cod
	OR cod
	OR halibut
	OR grouper
	OR other firm, mild-flavored fish
fish, sole	orange roughy
	OR flounder
	OR other delicate, flaky fish
fish, swordfish	tuna
	OR mako shark
	OR other firm, meaty fish
fish, trout	salmon
	OR other firm or distinctively flavored fish
fish, tuna	swordfish
	OR mako shark
	OR other firm, meaty fish
five-spice powder, Chinese	see page 45
flour, all-purpose 1 cup sifted	1 cup less 2 tbs. unsifted all-purpose flour
flour, all-purpose 1 cup unsifted	1⅛ cups cake flour
flour, bread 1 cup	1 cup all-purpose flour + 1 tbs. vital gluten
flour, cake 1 cup	1 cup less 2 tbs. all-purpose flour, sifted OR ⅞ all-purpose flour + 2 tbs. cornstarch *Sift together.*
flour, graham	whole wheat flour
flour, pastry	see cake flour

If You Don't Have	Use
flour, potato (potato starch) *for thickening* 1 tbs.	1 tbs. arrowroot OR 1 tbs. cornstarch OR 2½ tbs. flour
flour, self-rising	see page 45
flour *for thickening* 2½ tbs.	1 tbs. cornstarch OR 1 tbs. arrowroot OR 1 tbs. potato flour (potato starch)
flour, whole wheat 1 cup	2 tbs. wheat germ + ⅞ cup all-purpose flour
galangal	fresh ginger
game hen, Cornish	squab OR quail OR other game bird
ganache, chocolate	see page 45
garam masala	see page 45
garlic 1 small clove, finely minced	⅛ tsp. garlic powder
garlic powder ⅛ tsp.	1 small clove garlic, finely minced OR ¼ tsp. garlic salt *Omit salt in recipe.*
garlic salt	see page 45
ginger, fresh 1 tbs. chopped	⅛-¼ tsp. powdered ginger OR 1 tbs. chopped candied ginger *Rinse to remove sugar.*
glaze, fruit	melted jam OR fruit-flavored syrup, reduced slightly
goose	duck OR capon OR turkey OR other game bird

If You Don't Have	Use
Grand Marnier	Curaçao OR Cointreau OR Triple Sec OR orange juice concentrate
grapes, green	kiwi fruit
grapefruit	pomelo
grenadine	maraschino cherry juice
half-and-half	see cream
herb blends	see pages 45-46
herbes de Provence	see page 46
herbs, dried 1 tsp.	1 tbs. chopped fresh herbs
herbs, fresh 1 tbs. chopped	1 tsp. dried herbs
hominy, whole	white corn
hominy grits	white cornmeal
honey 1 cup	1¼ cups sugar + ¼ cup water *Reduce liquid in recipe by ¼ cup.*
Italian herb seasoning	see page 46
jicama	water chestnuts
kale *for cooking*	mustard greens OR collard greens OR turnip greens OR Swiss chard leaves
ketchup ¾ cup	¾ cup chili sauce OR ½ cup tomato sauce + 3 tbs. sugar + 1 tbs. white vinegar *Mix all ingredients together.*
kippers	sardines OR anchovies
kiwi fruit	green grapes

If You Don't Have	Use
kohlrabi	small, mild turnip
kumquats	tangerines *Do not use tangerine peels.*
ladyfingers	pound cake strips OR angel food cake strips OR sponge cake strips
lard ⅞ cup	1 cup vegetable shortening OR 1 cup butter OR 1 cup margarine
lentils	split peas
leeks	shallots OR green onions (scallions)
lemon juice, fresh	fresh lime juice
lemon juice from 1 lemon	3 tbs. bottled lemon juice
lemon juice 1 tsp.	½ tsp. vinegar
lemon grass	fresh lemon zest
lemon zest, fresh 1 tsp. minced	1 tsp. dried lemon peel OR 1 tsp. minced lemon grass
lime juice	lemon juice
lime juice from 1 lime	1½-2 tbs. bottled lime juice
lobster	monkfish (anglerfish) tail OR crab OR shrimp OR crayfish
lovage	celery leaves
mace, ground	ground nutmeg
mango	papaya OR cantaloupe

If You Don't Have	Use
margarine 1 cup	1 cup butter OR 1 cup vegetable shortening OR ⅞ cup lard
marjoram, fresh or dried	fresh or dried oregano
Marsala	sherry OR sweet white wine
mayonnaise	see page 46
melon, cantaloupe	honeydew or other melon OR mango OR papaya
milk *for baking*	fruit juice OR potato water
milk, evaporated	half-and-half OR heavy cream
milk, nonfat (skim) 1 cup	⅓ cup instant nonfat dry milk + ¾ cup water *Mix ingredients together.*
milk, sour 1 cup	1 tbs. lemon juice or white vinegar + milk to equal 1 cup *Let stand for 5 minutes.*
milk, sweetened, condensed 2 cups	4 cups nonfat (skim) milk + ¼ cup sugar *Bring milk to a boil in a heavy saucepan. Reduce heat to low and simmer, stirring, for about 30 minutes. Add sugar and simmer, stirring, until liquid has reduced to 2 cups.*
milk, whole 1 cup	½ cup evaporated whole milk + ½ cup water OR 1 cup puréed tofu OR ½ cup heavy cream + ½ cup water
mirin	see rice wine
molasses	dark corn syrup
mulling spices	see page 47

If You Don't Have	Use
mushrooms, fresh 1 lb.	3 oz. dried mushrooms, rehydrated *Bring 2 cups water to a boil. Add dried mushrooms, remove from heat and let stand for 20 to 30 minutes. Strain mushrooms and lightly squeeze out excess liquid. Use as you would fresh mushrooms. Depending on the dish, you can use stock, wine, milk or other flavorful soaking liquids; reserve the liquid for soups, sauces or for cooking rice.*
mushrooms, brown (cremini)	white mushrooms OR shiitake mushrooms OR portobello mushrooms
mushrooms, cremini	see brown mushrooms
mushrooms, portobello	brown (cremini) mushrooms
mushrooms, shiitake	brown (cremini) mushrooms OR portobello mushrooms
mushrooms, white	brown (cremini) mushrooms
mussels	clams OR oysters
mustard, prepared 1 tbs.	1 tsp. dry mustard in wet ingredients OR 1 tsp. dry mustard + ½ tsp. water + ¼ tsp. white vinegar *Mix ingredients together.*
mustard greens *for cooking*	dandelion greens OR Swiss chard leaves OR kale OR spinach
nectarines	peaches, peeled if desired OR apricots
nonstick cooking spray	vegetable oil in a spray bottle
noodles	wonton wrappers, cut into strips
nutmeg, ground	ground mace
nuts, almonds	pine nuts

If You Don't Have	Use
nuts, Brazil	hazelnuts OR walnuts OR pecans OR almonds
nuts, hazelnuts	Brazil nuts OR walnuts OR pecans OR almonds
nuts, pecans	walnuts OR hazelnuts OR almonds OR Brazil nuts
nuts, pine nuts	chopped almonds OR chopped walnuts OR chopped pistachio nuts
nuts, pistachio	pine nuts
nuts, walnuts	pecans OR hazelnuts OR almonds OR Brazil nuts
oil *for sautéing*	stock OR white wine OR apple juice OR water *Texture of sautéed item will be slightly different than if sautéed in oil.*
oil, canola	vegetable oil OR soybean oil OR safflower oil OR sunflower oil OR corn oil OR other mild-flavored oil
oil, Chinese chile	see page 47

If You Don't Have	Use
oil, corn	vegetable oil OR canola oil OR soybean oil OR safflower oil OR sunflower oil OR other mild-flavored oil
oil, sesame	see page 47
oil, safflower	vegetable oil OR soybean oil OR canola oil OR sunflower oil OR corn oil OR other mild-flavored oil
oil, soybean	vegetable oil OR safflower oil OR canola oil OR sunflower oil OR corn oil OR other mild-flavored oil
oil, sunflower	vegetable oil OR safflower oil OR canola oil OR soybean oil OR corn oil OR other mild-flavored oil
oil, vegetable	soybean oil OR safflower oil OR canola oil OR sunflower oil OR corn oil OR other mild-flavored oil
olives, green, full-flavored 1 tbs. chopped	1 tbs. capers
onion 1 cup chopped	1 tbs. dried minced onion, rehydrated *Pour 1/4 cup boiling water over onions and let stand for 15 minutes. Gently squeeze liquid from onions.* OR 1 cup chopped shallots

If You Don't Have	Use
onion 1 small, chopped	4 green onions (scallions), chopped
onions, green, white part 1 tbs. chopped	1 tbs. chopped shallots
onions, green, tops 1 tbs. chopped	1 tbs. chopped fresh chives
onion powder 1½ tsp.	½ medium onion, finely minced OR 1½ tsp. onion salt *Omit salt in recipe.*
onion salt	see page 47
orange sections, Mandarin	tangerine sections
orange zest, fresh 1 tsp. minced	1 tsp. dried orange peel
oregano, fresh or dried	fresh or dried marjoram
orzo	rice OR bulgur wheat OR couscous OR quinoa
oysters	mussels OR clams
pancake mix	see page 47
pancetta	bacon OR salt pork, for flavoring
papaya	mango OR cantaloupe
parsnips, cooked	cooked carrots OR cooked mild turnips
pasta, angel hair	cooked spaghetti squash
pasta, fettuccine	egg roll wrappers, cut into strips
peanut butter 1 cup	2 cups salted or unsalted peanuts *Blend with a food processor or blender until smooth.*
peaches	nectarines OR apricots

If You Don't Have	Use
pears, fresh or dried	fresh or dried apples
pea pods, snow	sugar snap peas
peas, split	lentils
peas, sugar snap	snow pea pods
pepper, black	white pepper OR paprika
pepper, cayenne ⅛ tsp.	3-4 drops hot pepper sauce, such as Tabasco OR ⅛ tsp. pure hot chile powder
peppers, red bell, roasted	pimientos
peppercress	watercress OR arugula
pepperoni	spicy salami OR sausage
pesto	see page 48
pheasant	goose OR quail OR squab OR other game bird
pickling spice	see page 48
pie crust	phyllo dough in several layers *Brush each layer with clarified or melted butter.* OR purchased puff pastry *Roll out pastry to fit pan; prick bottom of pastry several times with a fork.* OR see page 36
pimientos	roasted red bell peppers
pineapple	grapefruit OR oranges
plantains *for cooking*	green bananas
plums	apricots OR nectarines OR peaches

If You Don't Have	Use
polenta	cornmeal
pomelo	grapefruit
pork cutlets	flattened boneless chicken or turkey breasts OR veal cutlets
potatoes, sweet	butternut squash OR pumpkin
poultry seasoning	see page 48
prawns	large shrimp
prosciutto	cured, smoked ham, such as Virginia or Smithfield
prunes, chopped	raisins OR dried figs OR dates
pumpkin	butternut squash OR sweet potatoes
pumpkin pie spice	see page 48
quail	Cornish game hen OR squab OR other small game bird
quiche	see page 48
quinoa	rice OR bulgur wheat OR couscous
radishes	daikon radish
radicchio	Belgian endive
raisins	chopped prunes OR dried currants OR dried cherries OR dried cranberries
rice	orzo OR couscous OR quinoa OR bulgur wheat

If You Don't Have	Use
rice, Arborio	short-grain or "pearl" rice
rice, basmati	jasmine rice OR Texmati rice
rice, jasmine	basmati rice OR Texmati rice
rice, Texmati	jasmine rice OR basmati rice
rice wine (mirin)	dry sherry OR sake
rum	brandy OR cognac OR rum extract
saffron	turmeric
sake *for cooking*	rice wine (mirin) OR dry sherry
salad dressing, Caesar	see page 49
salad dressing, Russian	see page 49
salad dressing, Thousand Island	see page 49
salad dressing, vinaigrette	see page 49
salami	pepperoni
salsa, green	see page 49
salsa, red	see page 50
salt	lemon juice or vinegar to taste OR herb blends, pages 45-46 OR celery, garlic or onion salt
salt, seasoned	see page 50
salt pork *for flavoring*	bacon OR ham OR Canadian bacon OR pancetta
sardines	anchovies OR kippers

If You Don't Have	Use
sauce, barbecue	see page 50
sauce, brown, quick	see page 50
sauce, butterscotch	see page 51
sauce, caramel	see page 51
sauce, cheese	see page 51
sauce, cocktail	see page 51
sauce, custard (crème anglaise)	premium vanilla ice cream, melted OR see page 52
sauce, fudge, hot	see page 52
sauce, hard	see page 52
sauce, hollandaise	see page 53
sauce, horseradish	see page 53
sauce, hot pepper 3-4 drops	⅛ tsp. cayenne pepper OR ⅛ tsp. pure hot chile powder
sauce, mint	see page 53
sauce, rèmoulade	see page 53
sauce, spaghetti	see page 54
sauce, sweet and sour	see page 54
sauce, tartar	see page 54
sauce, tomato 1½ cups	1 can (6 oz.) tomato paste + ¾ cup water *Stir ingredients together until smooth.*
sauce, white, quick	see page 54
sauerkraut	shredded green cabbage
savory, summer, fresh or dried	fresh or dried thyme
shallots, chopped 3-4	1 medium onion, chopped OR 3-4 green onions, white part only, chopped
sherry, sweet	sweet white wine OR Marsala

If You Don't Have	Use
sherry, dry	rice wine (mirin) OR sake
shortening, vegetable 1 cup	1 cup butter OR 1 cup margarine OR ⅞ cup lard
shrimp	crayfish OR lobster OR crab
sour cream	see cream
spinach *for cooking*	Swiss chard leaves OR mustard greens
spinach *for salads*	romaine lettuce
squab	quail OR Cornish game hen OR other small game bird
squash, butternut	pumpkin OR acorn squash OR sweet potatoes
squash, pattypan	zucchini OR yellow crookneck squash
squash, yellow crookneck	zucchini OR pattypan squash
squash, zucchini	yellow crookneck squash OR pattypan squash OR eggplant
stock, beef or chicken 1 cup	1 bouillon cube or 1 tsp. bouillon granules + 1 cup boiling water *Mix ingredients together and stir until dissolved. Omit salt from recipe.* OR see page 55
stock, fish	clam juice OR see page 56

If You Don't Have		Use
sugar, brown 1/2 cup, packed	+	1/2 cup granulated sugar 2 tbs. molasses
sugar, confectioners' 1 cup	+	7/8 cup granulated sugar 1 tbs. cornstarch *Whirl in a blender for a few seconds.*
sugar, granulated 1 cup		3/4 cups confectioners' sugar
	OR	1 cup molasses *Reduce liquid in recipe by 1/3 cup.*
	OR	3/4 cup honey *Reduce liquid in recipe by 1/4 cup.*
	OR	1 cup turbinado (raw) sugar
	OR +	1/4 cup molasses 1/4 cup light corn syrup *Reduce liquid in recipe by 2 tbs.*
sugar, superfine		granulated sugar *Whirl in a blender for a few seconds.*
Swiss chard		see chard
syrup, for pancakes and waffles	+	1 part honey or brown sugar 1 part butter *Melt together.*
	OR +	3 parts molasses 1 part butter *Melt together.*
	OR	warmed applesauce or jam
syrup, simple		see page 56
taco seasoning		see page 56
tahini (sesame paste)	+	smooth peanut butter sesame oil to taste, optional
tamari		soy sauce
tamarind *for flavoring only*		lemon juice

If You Don't Have	Use
tangerines	oranges OR kumquats OR canned Mandarin orange sections, drained
tarragon, fresh	fennel fronds
thyme, fresh or dried	fresh or dried summer savory
tomatoes, canned 1 cup	1⅓ cups peeled, chopped fresh tomatoes with juice *Simmer in a skillet for a few minutes.*
tomatoes, fresh, chopped 1⅓ cups	1 cup chopped canned tomatoes
tomato juice 1 cup	½ cup tomato sauce + ½ cup water *Mix ingredients together.*
tomato puree 1 cup	½ cup tomato paste + ½ cup water *Mix ingredients together.*
tomato sauce 1½ cups	1 can (6 oz.) tomato paste + ¾ cup water *Stir ingredients together until smooth.*
tongue	corned beef OR pastrami OR ham OR bologna
treacle	molasses
Triple Sec	Grand Marnier OR Curaçao OR Cointreau OR orange juice concentrate
turnips	rutabagas OR kohlrabi
turnip greens *for cooking*	Swiss chard leaves OR kale OR beet greens OR collard greens
turmeric	saffron

If You Don't Have	Use
vanilla bean 1-inch piece	1 tsp. vanilla extract
vanilla extract 1 tsp.	1-inch piece vanilla bean
vanilla sugar	see page 56
veal cutlets (scalloppini)	flattened boneless chicken or turkey breasts OR pork cutlets
venison	beef OR buffalo
vermouth, dry	dry white wine
vinaigrette	see salad dressing
vinegar 1 tsp.	2 tsp. lemon juice
wasabi	prepared horseradish OR dry mustard mixed with water
water chestnuts	jicama
watercress	arugula OR peppercress
whiskey, blended	bourbon
wine, dry white *for cooking*	dry vermouth OR champagne
wine, dry white *for marinades* ½ cup	¼ cup vinegar + ¼ cup water + 1 tbs. sugar *Mix ingredients together.*
yeast, active dry 1 pkg.	1 scant tbs. yeast
yogurt, plain, for cooking	buttermilk
zucchini	see squash

If You Don't Have	Use

HEALTHY
SUBSTITUTIONS

Sometimes you want to adjust recipes so that they fit into a healthy lifestyle. For example:

- You need a healthy alternative to a high-fat and/or high-cholesterol ingredient.

- You are trying to cut down on sugar, salt and other excesses in you diet.

- You are feeding someone with special dietary needs.

This section is designed to address any of these issues. Use it as a guide when you wish to make a healthy substitution.

TIP: Remove excessive fat from the top of homemade or purchased soups by placing them in the refrigerator until completely cold. The fat will solidify and rise to the top and can be easily removed with a large spoon.

TIP: Use highly flavored foods, such as prosciutto, olives, capers, strong cheeses, garlic and horseradish to help replace some of the fat in your recipes. Although some of these items contain fat, a little of them goes a long way to flavor foods.

TIP: Use the blank chart at the back of the section to record your own healthy substitutions.

Instead of	Use
bacon, cooked	Canadian bacon OR turkey bacon OR soy bacon OR imitation bacon bits
beef	venison OR buffalo
beef, ground	ground turkey OR ground chicken OR ground buffalo OR ground venison
breadcrumbs, dry	toasted or untoasted wheat germ OR stale French bread *Process with a blender or food processor into crumbs.*
breads, high-fat	low-fat breads *Avoid breads that are high in fat and calories, such as croissants, brioche, egg bagels, etc. Instead, choose breads that are low in fat and calories, such as French or sourdough loaves, English muffins and non-egg bagels.*
breads, quick	yeast breads *Watch for high-fat ingredients.*
butter	margarine OR vegetable shortening OR vegetable oil OR applesauce, for baking OR apple or orange juice concentrate, for baking *Butter contains a high percentage of saturated fat and cholesterol. Vegetable-based margarine, vegetable shortening and vegetable oil have a lower percent of saturated fat. For more information, see oils.*
cake, pound	angel food cake
cheese	reduced-fat versions of purchased cheese OR full-flavored grating cheese, such as Parmesan or Romano *Although these cheeses contain high amounts of fat, a small amount goes a long way to flavor dishes.*

Instead of	Use
cheese, cream	yogurt cheese, page 41
	OR purchased low-fat or nonfat cream cheese *Do not cook over high heat.*
	OR domestic neufchatel cheese
cheese, ricotta	pureed low-fat cottage cheese OR nonfat cream cheese OR yogurt cheese, page 41 *Do not cook over high heat.*
chicken, dark meat with skin	white meat chicken without skin *Tip: cook chicken breasts with skin and remove skin just before eating. This helps the chicken stay juicy.*
chocolate	carob *Carob's fat and calories are similar to chocolate's, but carob contains no caffeine.*
	OR cocoa *Use recipes that contain pure cocoa instead of chocolate. These recipes will usually contain fewer calories and fat, but watch for added butter and oil. For a rich chocolate flavor, choose "Dutch-processed" cocoa. It may be a little more expensive than the regular version, but the results are well worth it.*
clams	see shellfish
coconut milk 1½ cups	1 cup nonfat yogurt + ½ cup nonfat milk + ½ tsp. coconut extract *Combine all ingredients; do not boil.*
cookies, high-fat	meringue cookies *Watch for high-fat additions, such as chocolate chips and/or nuts.*
	OR purchased gingersnaps, sugar wafers, animal crackers, fig or other fruit bars, graham crackers or vanilla wafers *Some brands contain more fat and calories than others. Check the labels for nutritional information.*
	OR low-fat or nonfat versions of purchased cookies

Instead of	Use
crab	see shellfish
crackers	melba toast OR flatbread OR lavosh OR matzo OR rice crackers OR baked tortilla wedges, page 38 OR baked pita bread wedges, page 38 *Avoid butter crackers and "flavored" crackers with extra sugars and fats.*
cream, heavy *for whipping*	very cold evaporated skim milk
cream, heavy *not for whipping*	evaporated skim milk OR low-fat or nonfat plain yogurt
cream, sour	low-fat or nonfat sour cream OR low-fat or nonfat plain yogurt OR buttermilk
crème fraiche	low-fat or nonfat plain yogurt
custard, for baking 1½ cups	½ cup egg substitute + 1 cup evaporated skim milk *Season with salt and pepper or sugar to taste, depending on the dish.*
eggs 2	½ cup egg substitute OR 4 egg whites OR ½ cup applesauce, for baking
fats	see oils
flour *for thickening* 2 tbs.	2 tsp. cornstarch OR 2 tsp. arrowroot *Bring cooking liquid to a boil. Whisk arrowroot or cornstarch with a small amount of cold water or cold cooking liquid until consistency is like heavy cream. Add mixture slowly to hot liquid, stirring constantly, until desired thickness is reached.*

Instead of	Use
ice cream	low-fat or nonfat frozen yogurt OR sorbet OR frozen fruit bars *Eat as is, or remove stick and whirl in a blender until smooth; freeze again, if desired.*
jam	purchased all-fruit spread OR fruit coulis, page 41
jelly	see jam
lard	vegetable shortening OR margarine
liqueur	apple or orange juice concentrate
lobster	see shellfish
mayonnaise	purchased low-fat or nonfat mayonnaise OR mustard OR nonfat cream cheese OR yogurt cheese, page 41 OR very ripe avocado *The fat in avocados is monounsaturated, which is better for you than the saturated and polyunsaturated fats found in mayonnaise. Avocados also have fewer calories than mayonnaise and no cholesterol. Use sparingly.*
mayonnaise, homemade	reduced-fat homemade mayonnaise *You can get good emulsification and flavor with about 1/2 to 2/3 of the oil in a standard mayonnaise recipe. Stop adding oil when mayonnaise reaches acceptable thickness and flavor.*
meats, high-fat cuts	low-fat cuts of meat *beef: round, eye of round, tenderloin, sirloin, flank* *buffalo: any cut* *lamb: leg* *pork: tenderloin* *veal: cutlet* *venison: any cut* *Remove all visible fat from meat before cooking.* OR reduced-fat versions of meats

Instead of	Use
milk, sweetened, condensed *purchased*	homemade sweetened condensed milk, page 17
milk, whole	fruit juice OR potato water OR pureed tofu
mussels	see shellfish
noodles, egg	see pasta
nuts, high-fat	lower-fat nuts *Pecans, walnuts, hazelnuts and pine nuts are relatively high in fat; almonds, cashews and pistachio nuts are relatively low in fat. For a different texture, but very little fat, choose chestnuts.*
oil	oil in a spray bottle *Use sparingly.* OR oil applied with a pastry brush *Use sparingly.* OR nonstick cooking spray *Use sparingly.* OR nonstick cookware *You may still need a light touch of oil for sautéing.* OR small amount of stock, apple juice or water for sautéing *The texture of the food will be slightly different than when sautéed in oil.*
pasta, egg, dried	dried pasta made without eggs OR cooked spaghetti squash
pasta, egg, homemade	homemade egg-white pasta *Substitute 2 egg whites for each egg in the recipe.*

Instead of	Use
pie crust	phyllo dough in several layers *Spray each layer lightly with clarified or melted butter, margarine, vegetable oil or water.* OR egg roll wrappers, for miniature pies or tartlets OR French bread dough or pizza crust, for savory pies OR parchment paper, for quiche *Omit crust and line quiche pan with parchment paper.*
popcorn, oil-popped	air-popped popcorn OR purchased low-fat microwave popcorn OR see potato chips
potato chips	purchased low-fat or low-salt potato chips OR pretzels OR baked tortilla wedges, page 38 OR baked pita bread wedges, page 38
potatoes, baked *with butter and sour cream*	baked potatoes with low-fat toppings *Instead of with butter and sour cream, top baked potatoes with yogurt cheese, page 41, chili or salsa.*
potatoes, French fried	baked potato wedges *Cut russet potatoes lengthwise into 6 to 8 wedges. Place wedges on a baking sheet and spray lightly with canola oil. Bake at 450° for about 15 to 20 minutes.*
potatoes, mashed *with cream and butter*	low-fat mashed potatoes *Use buttermilk and/or chicken stock instead of cream and butter.*
preserves	see jam
puff pastry	see pie crust

Instead of	Use
salad dressing, vinaigrette	reduced-fat vinaigrette *Reduce the ratio of oil to vinegar from 3:1 to 1:1. Add more oil only if needed, to taste. Use vinegars that are not harsh, such as balsamic vinegar, rice vinegar or champagne vinegar. Or, use lemon juice.* OR vinaigrette in a spray bottle *Pour standard vinaigrette into a clean spray bottle and spray lightly onto salad greens.* OR seasoned rice vinegar OR lemon juice
salt	lemon or lime juice OR vinegar OR herb blends, pages 45-46 OR marinate food before cooking
scallops	see shellfish
shellfish, high-calorie and high-cholesterol	low-calorie and low-cholesterol shellfish *Choose shellfish that are low in calories and cholesterol. Shrimp are relatively high in calories and cholesterol. Lobster and crab are lower in calories and cholesterol; clams, scallops and mussels are even lower.*
shrimp	see shellfish
soup, cream-based	broth-based soup *For thickening, remove a portion of the vegetables, beans and/or potatoes from soup and puree with a food processor or blender. Return pureed mixture to soup and stir until blended.*
sugar, refined	fresh fruit purees OR apple or orange juice concentrate OR honey
tortillas, flour	corn tortillas OR purchased low-fat or nonfat flour tortillas

Instead of	**Use**
tortilla chips	baked tortilla wedges *Cut corn or flour tortillas into sixths and spray very lightly with water. Place on a baking sheet and bake at 375° for 8 to 10 minutes, or until browned and crisp, turning once. If desired, sprinkle with a small amount of lime juice and/or salt before baking.* OR baked pita bread wedges *Follow instructions for baked tortilla wedges, but bake for a few minutes longer.*
tuna, canned, oil-packed	water-packed canned tuna
vinaigrette	see salad dressing
yogurt, with added fruit	plain or vanilla nonfat yogurt with chopped fresh fruit *Add your own fruit to plain yogurt for less sugar and no extra processing.*

This section is especially helpful for cooks who like to improvise. For example:

- You don't have an ingredient in the pantry and can't get to the market to purchase it.

- You want a flavorful, fresh and inexpensive version of an herb and/or spice blend using ingredients you already have on hand in the kitchen cupboard.

- You want to know how to make a common sauce, but don't want to search your cookbook library for the recipe.

This section is designed to address any of these issues. While many of the suggestions save time and effort, some require extra time and preparation. Read the instructions carefully before beginning.

TIP: Some of the formulas are written in parts. Divide the amount you need by the total number of parts to obtain the amount needed per part.

To Make		Use
aioli about 1 cup	 + + +	1 cup mayonnaise 2-4 cloves garlic, very finely minced lemon juice to taste, optional salt and pepper to taste *If using homemade mayonnaise, make it with olive oil.*
almond paste *for fillings*	 + + + +	½ cup water 1 cup sugar 3 tbs. orange juice or rose water 8 oz. ground almonds confectioners' sugar *In a heavy saucepan, bring water and sugar to a boil and cook until mixture registers 240° on a candy thermometer (soft ball stage). Remove from heat. Add juice and almonds and stir until creamy. Let mixture stand until cool enough to handle. Transfer mixture to a board dusted with confectioners' sugar and knead briefly. Store in an airtight container and let stand for several days before using to develop flavors.*
apple pie spice	 + + +	2 parts cinnamon 1 part ground nutmeg 1 part ground allspice 1 part ground cardamom *Mix all ingredients together. Proportions can be altered to taste.*
beurre manie *for thickening*	 +	1 part butter, softened 1 part flour *Mix ingredients until well blended.*
biscuit mix 6-10 biscuits	 + + +	2 cups all-purpose flour 3 tsp. baking powder ½ tsp. salt 6 tbs. butter, margarine, vegetable shortening or lard, cut into pieces *In a bowl, mix together flour, baking powder and salt. Cut in butter with a pastry blender until mixture resembles cornmeal. To make biscuits, stir in ¾-1 cup milk until just moistened. Drop mixture onto a lightly greased baking sheet and bake at 450° for about 12 to 15 minutes, until golden brown.*

To Make	Use
blackening spices	10 parts paprika
	+ 8 parts salt
	+ 4 parts onion powder
	+ 4 parts garlic powder
	+ 4 parts cayenne pepper
	+ 3 parts black pepper
	+ 3 parts white pepper
	+ 3 parts dried thyme
	+ 2 parts dried oregano
	Combine all ingredients. Rub mixture over the surface of meat, poultry or fish. Let stand at room temperature for 1 hour, or refrigerate for longer, before cooking.
bouquet garni	1 bay leaf
	+ 1 sprig fresh thyme
	+ 3 sprigs fresh parsley
	Tie together with kitchen string.
butter, clarified 6 oz.	8 oz. unsalted butter
	Melt butter very slowly in a saucepan over low heat until the milk solids separate and sink to the bottom. Skim the foam that rises to the top and discard. Very carefully pour off just the golden liquid.
butter, maitre d'hotel about ½ cup	½ cup unsalted butter, softened
	+ 1 tsp. salt
	+ 2 drops hot pepper sauce, such as Tabasco, optional
	+ 1 tbs. fresh lemon juice
	+ 1 tbs. chopped fresh parsley
	In a small bowl, whip butter until smooth. Add remaining ingredients and mix well. Place butter in a ramekin, or form into a log and wrap with plastic wrap. Refrigerate until ready to serve.
Cajun spice blend	8 parts dried minced onion
	+ 2 parts garlic powder
	+ 2 parts celery salt
	+ 2 parts black pepper
	+ 2 parts dried thyme
	+ 2 parts dry mustard
	+ 1 part cayenne pepper
	Mix all ingredients together.

To Make	Use
cheese, yogurt 1 cup	2 cups nonfat, plain, gelatin-free yogurt *Place yogurt in a yogurt drainer, or in a colander lined with a paper coffee filter suspended over a bowl. Cover and refrigerate overnight. Discard the liquid that exudes.*
chili powder	8 parts ground dried chile peppers + 4 parts ground cumin + 3 parts paprika + 2 parts garlic powder + 1 part dried oregano + 1 part cayenne pepper, or more to taste *Mix all ingredients together.*
chili sauce about 1½ cups	2 cups chopped canned tomatoes + ½ onion, chopped + ¼ cup cider vinegar + 2 tbs. brown sugar + ½ tsp. salt + ⅛ tsp. ground cloves + ⅛ tsp. cinnamon + ¼ cup minced green bell pepper *In a saucepan, simmer all ingredients, except bell pepper, for 1 hour; add pepper and simmer for 30 additional minutes. Puree if desired.*
cinnamon sugar	9 parts sugar + 1 part cinnamon *Mix ingredients together.*
cocoa mix, hot 10 servings	1 cup sugar + ½ cup unsweetened cocoa powder + 1 cup instant nonfat dry milk + 1 tsp. cinnamon, optional + 1 tsp. instant espresso or coffee powder, optional *Mix all ingredients together. For each serving, stir ¼ cup mix into ¾ cup boiling water.*
coulis, fruit or vegetable about 1 cup	2 cups chopped fruits or vegetables lemon juice to taste, optional sugar, honey or salt to taste, optional *Puree fruit or vegetables with a blender and press through a mesh strainer. Or, process fruits or vegetables with a food mill. Stir in remaining ingredients.*

To Make	Use
court-bouillon about 5 cups	1 qt. water + 1½ cups dry white wine + 1 onion, coarsely chopped + 1 carrot, sliced + 2 stalks celery, chopped + 1 sprig fresh parsley + 6 whole peppercorns + 1 bay leaf + ½ tsp. salt *Combine all ingredients in a saucepan and simmer for about 30 minutes; strain.*
crab boil	1 part crushed bay leaves + 1 part peppercorns + 1 part coriander seeds + 1 part whole cloves + 1 part whole allspice + 1 part mustard seeds + 1 part dill seeds + 1 part red pepper flakes *Mix all ingredients together.*
crème anglaise	see sauce, custard
crème chantilly about 2 cups	1 cup cold heavy cream + 2 tbs. superfine sugar + ¾ tsp. vanilla extract, liquor or liqueur *Whip cream until soft peaks form. While whipping, gradually add sugar and vanilla and whip until desired consistency is reached.*
crème fraiche about 1⅛ cups	1 cup lukewarm heavy cream + 2 tbs. buttermilk *Mix ingredients together in a nonmetallic container. Cover and let stand at room temperature overnight. Refrigerate until ready to use.*

To Make	Use
Creole seasoning	3 parts paprika + 2 parts cayenne pepper + 1 part black pepper + 1 part white pepper + 1 part dried oregano + 1 part dried thyme + 1 part garlic powder + 1 part onion powder + 1 part salt *Mix all ingredients together.*
curry powder	6 parts ground coriander + 4 parts ground cumin + 4 parts ground fenugreek seeds + 2 parts ground ginger + 2 parts ground mustard seeds + 2 parts turmeric + 4 parts black pepper + 1 part cinnamon + 1 part ground red pepper flakes, or more to taste *Mix all ingredients together.*
custard *for baking* 1½ quarts	8 eggs, beaten, or 2 cups egg substitute + 1 qt. cream or milk + sugar or seasonings to taste *Mix all ingredients together.*
dry rub for beef or lamb about ½ cup	¼ cup dried rosemary + 1 tbs. dried thyme + 1 tbs. crushed cumin seeds or ground cumin + 1 tbs. black pepper + 2 tsp. salt + ½ tsp. garlic powder *Mix all ingredients together and rub over the surface of meat. Let stand at room temperature for 1 hour, or in the refrigerator for longer, before grilling, roasting or broiling.*

To Make	Use
dry rub for fish about 1 cup	½ cup dried dill weed + ¼ cup dried lemon peel + 3 tbs. paprika + 1 tbs. white pepper + 1 tbs. cayenne pepper + 1 tsp. salt *Mix all ingredients together and rub over the surface of fish. Let stand at room temperature for 1 hour, or in the refrigerator for longer, before grilling, roasting or broiling.*
dry rub for pork about ½ cup	¼ cup dried thyme ¼ cup dried orange peel + 2 tbs. dried sage + 2 tsp. black pepper + 1 tsp. salt + ½ tsp. onion powder *Mix all ingredients together and rub over the surface of pork. Let stand at room temperature for 1 hour, or in the refrigerator for longer, before grilling, roasting or broiling.*
dry rub for poultry about ½ cup	¼ cup dried lemon peel + 1 tbs. dried thyme + 1 tbs. dried basil + 1 tbs. dried marjoram + 1 tbs. ground black pepper + 2 tsp. salt *Mix all ingredients together and rub over the surface of poultry. Let stand at room temperature for 1 hour, or in the refrigerator for longer, before grilling, roasting or broiling.*
fines herbes, fresh or dried	1 part minced chervil + 1 part minced chives + 1 part minced parsley + 1 part minced tarragon *Mix all ingredients together. If fresh, add to dish shortly before serving. If dried, add to dish and simmer to develop flavors.*

To Make	Use
five-spice powder, Chinese	1 part cinnamon + 1 part ground cloves + 1 part ground fennel seeds + 1 part ground star anise + 1 part ground Szechwan peppercorns *If necessary, grind whole spices with a coffee mill, spice grinder or mortar and pestle before measuring. Mix all ingredients together.*
flour, self-rising about 1 cup	1 cup all-purpose flour + 1½ tsp. baking powder + ⅛ tsp. salt *Sift ingredients together.*
ganache, chocolate about 3 cups	1½ cups heavy cream + 12 oz. semisweet chocolate, chopped + 1 tbs. vanilla extract, liquor or liqueur *In a heavy saucepan, bring cream to a simmer, add chocolate and stir until smooth. Remove from heat and stir in flavoring. For a glaze, cool mixture to lukewarm and pour over item to be glazed. For a filling, refrigerate mixture until cold; whip until stiff and creamy.*
garam masala	4 parts cumin seeds + 2 parts crushed cinnamon stick + 2 parts black peppercorns + 2 parts cardamom pods + 1 part whole cloves *With a spice grinder or electric coffee mill, grind spices together until powdery.*
garlic salt	1 part garlic powder + 4 parts salt *Mix ingredients together.*
herb blend for beef dishes	1 part dried rosemary + 1 part dried thyme + 1 part dried minced garlic *Mix all ingredients together.*
herb blend for lamb dishes	1 part dried parsley + 1 part cup dried mint + 1 part dried minced garlic *Mix all ingredients together.*

To Make	Use
herb blend for fish dishes	2 parts dried chives + 2 parts dried parsley + 2 parts dried dill *Mix all ingredients together.*
herb blend for poultry dishes	1 part dried chives + 1 part dried parsley + 1 part dried tarragon *Mix all ingredients together.*
herb blend for pork dishes	1 part dried sage + 1 part dried thyme + 1 part dried rosemary *Mix all ingredients together.*
herbes de Provence	3 parts dried basil + 3 parts dried rosemary + 3 parts dried thyme + 2 parts dried summer savory + 1 part dried lavender *Mix all ingredients together.*
Italian herb seasoning	1 part dried basil + 1 part dried marjoram + 1 part dried oregano + 1 part dried sage *Mix all ingredients together.*
mayonnaise 1 cup	2 egg yolks or 1 egg* + 2 tbs. white vinegar or lemon juice + ¼ tsp. salt + 1 cup vegetable or olive oil *With a blender or food processor, process yolks, vinegar and salt until smooth. With machine running, slowly add oil and blend until thick and creamy.* ** Some health authorities discourage using raw eggs in recipes due to possible bacterial contamination.*

To Make		Use
mulling spices for 1 quart cider or wine	 + + +	2 sticks cinnamon 2 tsp. whole cloves zest of 1 orange sugar to taste, optional *Simmer ingredients with 1 quart cider or wine for about 15 minutes; strain.*
oil, Chinese chile about 1 cup	 +	6 small dried red chile peppers 1 cup vegetable oil *Place chiles and oil in a small saucepan and bring to a boil. Stir mixture and continue to boil for 5 to 30 seconds, depending on desired strength. Cool completely and strain.*
oil, sesame about ½ cup	 +	½ cup vegetable oil 2 tbs. sesame seeds *In a saucepan, slightly heat oil; add seeds, cool to room temperature and transfer to a jar with a tight-fitting lid. Store in a cool, dark place for 2 to 3 days; strain before using.*
onion salt	 +	1 part onion powder 1 part salt *Mix ingredients together.*
pancake mix 8-12 pancakes, depending on size	 + + + +	2 cups all-purpose flour 1 tbs. baking powder ½ tsp. salt 1 tbs. sugar 6 tbs. butter, margarine or vegetable shortening, cut into small pieces *In a bowl, mix together flour, baking powder, salt and sugar. Cut in butter with a pastry blender until mixture resembles cornmeal. To make pancakes, stir in 1 beaten egg, or ¼ cup egg substitute, and 1¼ cups milk or buttermilk until just moistened. Ladle mixture onto a hot griddle and cook until golden brown on both sides and cooked through.*

To Make	Use
pesto	1 cup chopped fresh basil or other fresh herb + 2 cloves garlic, minced + ¼ cup chopped pine nuts or walnuts + ½ cup grated Parmesan or Romano cheese + salt to taste + ⅓ cup extra virgin olive oil *Process all ingredients, except olive oil, with a blender or food processor until smooth. With machine running, add oil in a thin stream and blend until well mixed.*
pickling spice	8 parts mustard seeds + 4 parts crushed bay leaves + 2 parts crushed cinnamon stick + 2 parts black peppercorns + 2 parts whole allspice + 1 part red pepper flakes + 1 part whole cloves *Mix all ingredients together.*
poultry seasoning	1 part dried sage + 1 part dried thyme + 1 part dried marjoram + 1 part dried summer savory *Mix all ingredients together.*
pumpkin pie spice	4 parts ground cinnamon + 2 parts ground ginger + 1 part ground nutmeg + 1 part ground allspice *Mix all ingredients together. Proportions can be altered to taste.*
quiche one 9-inch quiche	4 eggs, beaten, or 1 cup egg substitute + 2 cups cream or milk + 1-2 cups diced vegetables, diced meat and/or shredded cheese + herbs and spices to taste + salt and pepper to taste *Combine all ingredients and mix well. Pour mixture into a pastry-lined pie pan and bake at 375° for 35 to 45 minutes, until eggs are set.*

To Make		Use
salad dressing, Caesar about 1½ cups	 + + + + + + +	1 cup olive oil 4 cloves garlic, minced ¼ cup lemon juice 2 tbs. wine vinegar 2 tbs. grated imported Parmesan cheese 1 tbs. mashed anchovies, optional dash Worcestershire sauce, optional dash hot pepper sauce, such as Tabasco, optional salt and freshly ground pepper to taste *Blend or whisk ingredients together.*
salad dressing, Russian about 1½ cups	 + + + +	1 cup mayonnaise ¼ cup chili sauce 1 tbs. horseradish 1 tbs. minced onion salt and pepper to taste *Blend or whisk ingredients together.*
salad dressing, Thousand Island about 1⅔ cups	 + + + +	1 cup mayonnaise ¼ cup chili sauce 2 tbs. chopped onion 2 tbs. chopped green bell pepper 1 hard-cooked egg, chopped, optional salt and pepper to taste *Blend or whisk ingredients together.*
salad dressing, vinaigrette about ⅔ cup	 + + + +	6 tbs. olive oil 2 tbs. balsamic or red wine vinegar 1 tsp. Dijon mustard, optional ⅛ tsp. salt pinch black pepper 1 small shallot, minced *Blend or whisk ingredients together.*
salsa, green about 1¼ cups	 + + + + + +	1 cup tomatillos, peeled and diced ½ onion, chopped 1 clove garlic, minced 2 tbs. chopped fresh cilantro 1 jalapeño or serrano chile, minced 1 tbs. lime juice salt to taste *Puree all ingredients with a blender or food processor.* *Let stand for about 15 minutes to blend flavors.*

To Make	Use
salsa, red about 1¼ cups	1 cup diced tomatoes with juice + 2 tbs. minced onion + 1 small clove garlic, minced, optional + 2 tsp. finely chopped fresh cilantro + 1 jalapeño or serrano chile, minced + 1½ tsp. lime juice + salt to taste *Combine all ingredients. Let stand for about 15 minutes to blend flavors.*
salt, seasoned about 1⅛ cups	1 cup salt + 2 tsp. paprika + 1 tsp. onion powder + 1 tsp. dried oregano + 1 tsp. garlic powder + ½ tsp. black pepper *Mix all ingredients together.*
sauce, barbecue about 3½ cups	1 large onion, minced + 2 cloves garlic, minced + 2 cups ketchup + ½ cup cider vinegar + ¾ cup water + 2 tbs. brown sugar + 1 tbs. Worcestershire sauce + 2 tsp. dry mustard + ½ tsp. black pepper + dash cayenne pepper + dash Liquid Smoke, optional *Mix all ingredients together until well blended.*
sauce, brown, quick about 1 cup	2 tbs. flour + 2 tbs. butter + 1¼ cups beef stock + bouquet garni, page 40 + salt and pepper to taste *In a skillet, stir flour with butter over medium heat for 2 minutes. Whisk in stock, reduce heat to low and simmer until thickened. Season with salt and pepper. Remove and discard bouquet garni.*

To Make	Use
sauce, butterscotch about 2⁄3 cup	½ cup light corn syrup + ½ cup light or dark brown sugar, packed + 2 tbs. butter + ¼ cup heavy cream + ½ tsp. vanilla extract *In a saucepan, bring corn syrup, brown sugar and butter to a boil. Reduce heat to low and simmer for 5 to 8 minutes, until mixture reaches a heavy, syrup-like consistency. Cool mixture slightly and stir in cream and vanilla.*
sauce, caramel about 1½ cups	¼ cup water + 1 cup sugar + 2⁄3 cup heavy cream, warmed *In a heavy saucepan, combine water and sugar. Cook over medium heat, stirring until sugar is dissolved. Increase heat to high and boil mixture, without stirring, until it turns amber in color. Remove from heat and slowly add cream. Return mixture to low heat and stir until smooth. Be very careful: the mixture is extremely hot.*
sauce, cheese about 1¼ cups	1 cup quick white sauce, page 54 + ¼ cup grated or crumbled cheese, such as cheddar, Parmesan, blue or other full-flavored cheese *In a small saucepan, heat white sauce over medium-low heat until just below the boiling point. Remove from heat and stir in cheese until smooth and melted.*
sauce, cocktail about 1¼ cups	1 cup ketchup or chili sauce + ¼ cup prepared horseradish + 2 tbs. lemon juice + 1-2 dashes hot pepper sauce, such as Tabasco *Mix all ingredients together until blended.*

To Make	Use
sauce, custard (crème anglaise) about 2¾ cups	2 cups heavy cream, half-and-half or milk + 6 egg yolks + ½ cup sugar + 1-2 tbs. vanilla extract *In a nonaluminum saucepan, heat cream until just below the boiling point. In a bowl, whip yolks and sugar with a whisk until light yellow in color. Ladle a small amount of hot cream into bowl with yolks, whisking constantly. Pour mixture in bowl into saucepan, whisking constantly. Stir mixture with a wooden spoon over low heat until sauce thickens and coats the back of spoon; do not boil or sauce will separate. Strain if desired. Stir in vanilla and serve warm. Or, cool sauce over an ice bath, stirring constantly, and serve cold.*
sauce, fudge, hot about 2 cups	2 tbs. butter + 4 oz. semisweet chocolate, chopped + 1 cup water + 2 cups sugar + ¼ cup light corn syrup + 1 tsp. vanilla extract *In a saucepan, melt butter with chocolate over low heat; set aside. In another saucepan, combine water, sugar and corn syrup and stir over medium heat until sugar is dissolved. Bring mixture to a boil and boil for 1 minute. Cool mixture slightly and stir in chocolate mixture. Return mixture to heat and boil for 5 minutes. Cool and add vanilla. If you want sauce to harden over ice cream, boil for 3 additional minutes.*
sauce, hard about 1 cup	⅓ cup butter, softened + 1 cup confectioners' sugar, sifted + pinch salt + 1 tbs. brandy or rum + ¼ cup heavy cream *With a mixer, beat butter until light and fluffy. Add sugar, a little at a time, and beat until well blended. Add salt, brandy and cream and mix until very smooth. Transfer to a storage container and refrigerate until ready to use.*

To Make		Use
sauce, hollandaise about ¾ cup	 + + + +	3 egg yolks* 2 tbs. lemon juice ¼ tsp. salt pinch cayenne pepper ½ cup butter, melted, kept warm *Combine all ingredients, except butter, in a blender container. With machine running, add butter slowly and blend until smooth and creamy. Serve immediately.* **Some health authorities discourage using undercooked eggs in recipes due to possible bacterial contamination.*
sauce, horseradish about 1¼ cups	 + + + +	1 cup softly whipped cream or sour cream, or ½ cup each mayonnaise and sour cream ¼ cup prepared horseradish 1 tbs. white vinegar 1 tsp. mustard salt to taste *Mix all ingredients until well blended. Refrigerate until ready to use.*
sauce, mint about ¾ cup	 + + + +	¼ cup water 2 tbs. confectioners' sugar 2 tbs. white vinegar or malt vinegar ¼ cup finely chopped fresh mint salt to taste *In a saucepan, bring water, sugar and vinegar to a boil; add mint and reduce heat to low. Cook until mixture is reduced and slightly thickened; strain if desired.*
sauce, rémoulade about 1¼ cups	 + + + + + +	1 cup mayonnaise 2 tbs. minced fresh chives or green onion tops 1 tbs. minced sweet pickle 1 tbs. chopped capers 1 tbs. chopped fresh parsley 2 tsp. mustard ½ tsp. dried tarragon *Mix all ingredients until well blended.*

To Make	Use
sauce, spaghetti about 1½ cups	1 medium onion, finely chopped + 2-3 cloves garlic, minced + ¼ cup olive oil + 2 cups chopped fresh or canned tomatoes + ½ cup tomato paste + ½ cup beef stock, optional + ¼ cup red wine, optional + 1 tsp. dried basil + 1 tsp. dried oregano + salt and pepper to taste *In a skillet, sauté onion and garlic in oil until soft. Stir in remaining ingredients and simmer for 30 to 45 minutes.*
sauce, sweet and sour about 1 cup	½ cup pineapple juice + ¼ cup ketchup + 2 tbs. brown sugar + ¼ cup vinegar + 1 tbs. cornstarch + 1 tsp. soy sauce *Combine all ingredients in a saucepan and bring to a boil. Reduce heat to low and simmer until slightly thickened. Serve warm or cold.*
sauce, tartar about 1¼ cups	1 cup mayonnaise + ¼ cup chopped sweet pickles + 2 tbs. lemon juice + 1 tbs. chopped onion + 1 tbs. chopped capers + dash cayenne pepper + salt to taste *Mix all ingredients until well blended.*
sauce, white, quick about 1 cup	2 tbs. flour + 2 tbs. butter + 1¼ cups milk + bouquet garni, page 40 + pinch nutmeg + salt and pepper to taste *In a skillet, stir flour with butter over medium heat for 2 minutes. Reduce heat to low, whisk in milk, add bouquet garni and and simmer until thickened. Season with nutmeg, salt and pepper. Remove and discard bouquet garni.*

To Make	Use
stock, beef about 12 cups	¼ cup olive oil + 2 onions, chopped + 2 carrots, chopped + 2 stalks celery, chopped + 4-5 lb. beef bones, browned if desired* + 1 gal. cold water + 2 sprigs fresh thyme + 2 sprigs fresh Italian parsley + 1 bay leaf + 6 black peppercorns *In a large pot, heat oil over medium heat and sauté vegetables until translucent. Add remaining ingredients and bring to a boil over high heat. Reduce heat to low and simmer for about 4 hours, skimming and discarding the foam that rises to the top. Strain stock and discard solids. Cool stock to room temperature and refrigerate overnight. Remove the layer of fat on top of cold stock before using.* **Browned bones will make a richer colored and flavored stock.*
stock, chicken about 12 cups	¼ cup olive oil + 2 onions, chopped + 2 carrots, chopped + 2 stalks celery, chopped + 4-5 lb. chicken bones, browned if desired* + 1 gal. cold water + 2 sprigs fresh thyme + 2 sprigs fresh Italian parsley + 1 bay leaf + 6 black peppercorns *In a large pot, heat oil over medium heat and sauté vegetables until translucent. Add remaining ingredients and bring to a boil over high heat. Reduce heat to low and simmer for 2 to 3 hours, skimming and discarding the foam that rises to the top. Strain stock and discard solids. Cool stock to room temperature and refrigerate overnight. Remove the layer of fat on top of cold stock before using.* **Browned bones will make a richer colored and flavored stock.*

To Make	Use
stock, fish about 8 cups	4 lb. bones and heads from mild white fish + 8 cups water + 1 medium onion, sliced + 1 sprig fresh Italian parsley + ½ lemon + 1 cup dry white wine + 6 white peppercorns + bouquet garni, page 40 *Place all ingredients in a large pot and bring to a boil over high heat. Reduce heat to low and simmer for about 30 minutes, skimming and discarding the foam that rises to the top. Strain stock, discard solids and cool to room temperature. Refrigerate until needed.*
syrup, simple	1 part sugar + 1 part water *Stir over medium heat until sugar is dissolved. Cool completely.*
taco seasoning	4 parts pure chile powder + 4 parts dried Mexican oregano + 2 parts salt + 2 parts onion powder + 2 parts ground cumin + 1 part garlic powder + 1 part black pepper *Mix all ingredients together.*
vanilla sugar about 2 cups	1 vanilla bean, split lengthwise + 2 cups sugar *Place vanilla bean and sugar in a jar with a tight-fitting lid. Let stand in a cool, dark place for at least 2 weeks.*
vinaigrette	see salad dressing

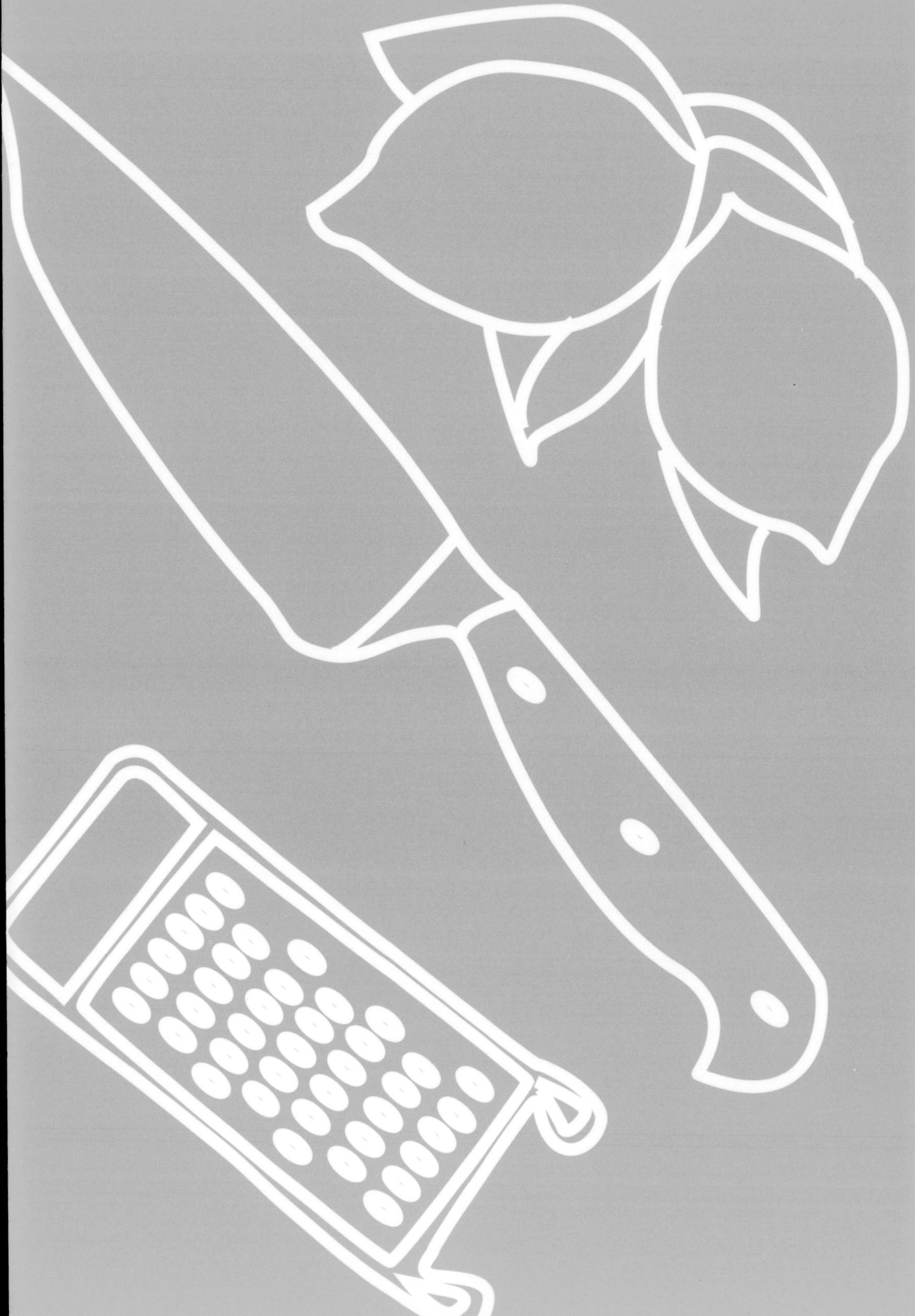

COOKING TOOLS

This section is a boon to cooks who are working with a sparsely equipped kitchen. For example:

- You want to make a recipe that calls for a certain piece of kitchen equipment, but don't want to purchase the equipment just to make the recipe.

- You are cooking in a friend's kitchen and don't have the right cooking tool for the job.

- You are planning a weekend getaway and don't wish to tote a great deal of cooking tools.

This section is designed to address any of these issues. Use it as a reminder of the versatility of many different kitchen items.

TIP: Use the blank chart at the back of the section to record your own alternative uses for kitchen tools.

If You Don't Have	Use
barbecue grill	oven shelf *Weight the corners with stones.*
cake slicer	kitchen twine OR unwaxed dental floss *Hold the ends of string and gently saw through cake vertically or horizontally.*
cheese shaver	vegetable peeler
cheesecloth *for straining*	piece of a sheet or pillowcase OR flat-weave dishtowel OR paper coffee filter
chocolate shaver	vegetable peeler OR grater
citrus stripper	vegetable peeler
citrus zester	vegetable peeler *Remove strips from the colored part of citrus peel.* *Mince strips with a knife.*
cleaver or large knife cover	plastic spine from a plastic report folder *Remove spine and trim to the length of knife or cleaver blade. Slip spine over knife blade to keep the edges sharp, as well as to prevent injury when not in use.*
coffee filter	heavy, "fancy" white paper napkin
cookie cutter	glass or plastic drinking glass *A plastic glass may have a sharper edge.*
cookie press	child's clay-extruding toy *Cut slices as they are pressed through.*
cooling rack	oven shelf OR grates from a gas stove OR elevated splatter screen, for light items
corn holders	toothpicks *Insert the pointed ends of toothpicks into the ends of corn ears.*
crockery pot	casserole or Dutch oven with a tight-fitting lid *Bake dish in a 200° oven for 8 hours.*

If You Don't Have		Use
double boiler		heatproof bowl set over a pan of simmering water
		Make sure water does not touch bowl. Use a potholder to hold the side of bowl while whisking or stirring.
egg beater		whisk
	OR	2 forks
		Turn tines in towards each other; hold tightly.
egg poacher		tuna-type cans in a skillet
		Cut the tops from empty, clean, shallow cans and arrange in skillet. Crack eggs into cans and carefully pour water about halfway up the sides of cans. Cook eggs until desired doneness and remove with a spatula.
egg slicer		pastry blender
fish poacher		Dutch oven with tight-fitting lid
		Place over 2 burners.
funnel		parchment paper
	OR	aluminum foil
		Roll parchment paper or aluminum foil into a cone shape. Insert cone into container and carefully pour liquid through cone into container.
insulated baking sheet		2 same-sized baking sheets
		Stack sheets on top of each other.
jelly bag		colander lined with cheesecloth
		Place several layers of cheesecloth inside colander and pour jelly mixture into cavity.
kitchen twine		unwaxed, unflavored dental floss
lid *for saucepans, casseroles, etc.*		aluminum foil
	OR	baking sheet
lid, transparent		glass pie pan

If You Don't Have	Use
meat mallet	hammer OR rolling pin OR skillet *Place meat between 2 pieces of waxed paper or plastic wrap. Use rolling pin, hammer or the bottom of skillet to flatten meat.*
mold *for salads and desserts*	stainless steel bowl
mortar and pestle *for dry items*	electric coffee mill OR heavy saucepan OR drinking glass *Place item to be crushed on a stable cutting board and crush item using the bottom of saucepan or glass.*
oyster shucker	pointed end of a bottle/can opener
parchment paper	brown paper OR waxed paper (do not use over high heat) OR greased and floured pan
pastry bag *for sturdy items*	plastic bag, preferably a sturdy locking type *Fill bag, remove excessive air from bag and seal tightly. With sharp scissors, snip a hole of desired size in the corner of bag and squeeze slowly and carefully. If you want to use a pastry tip, snip a hole in bag, insert tip, fill with desired filling and proceed.*
pastry bag *for delicate items*	parchment paper *For decorative items, such as melted chocolate or royal icing, roll parchment paper into a cone. Secure with transparent tape if desired. Fill bag, snip a very small hole in pointed end of cone and pipe item.*
pastry blender	2 forks or knives *Use a cutting motion to mix ingredients to desired consistency.* OR food processor *Pulse ingredients until desired consistency is reached; take care not to overmix.*

If You Don't Have	Use
pastry brush	oil or melted butter in a spray bottle *Spray oil or butter over surface to be brushed.*
pepper mill	electric coffee mill OR mortar and pestle OR heavy skillet *Crush peppercorns on a stable cutting board with the bottom of skillet.*
pie weights *for baking unfilled pie shells*	uncooked dried beans or rice *Line pastry with aluminum foil before adding beans.*
pizza cutter	kitchen shears OR large chef's knife
popover pan	muffin pan OR custard cups OR ramekins
potholder	folded dish towel OR restaurant-style tongs, for light items
potato masher	whisk OR large serving fork OR mixer *Take care not to overmix.*
rolling pin	wooden dowel OR wine bottle OR jar
spatula *for serving*	large putty knife
spatula *for spreading*	small putty knife
shaker *for dusting*	mesh strainer OR jar with a tight-fitting lid *With a nail and a hammer, punch several small holes into lid.* OR jar and cheesecloth *Place dusting ingredient inside jar. Cover jar with cheesecloth and secure tightly with a rubber band.*

If You Don't Have	Use
shrimp deveiner	pointed end of a bottle/can opener OR small scissors
skewer *for testing doneness*	see toothpick
sifter	wire mesh strainer *Fill strainer with flour or other item and tap lightly with a utensil or against your hand.*
spaetzle maker	colander *Press batter through holes in colander and snip or cut into 1- to 1½-inch pieces.*
steamer	stainless steel colander and pot *Make sure colander fits inside pot and pot lid fits securely.* OR heatproof plate, metal trivet and pot *If you don't have a trivet, use an empty tuna-type can with both ends removed. Make sure plate fits inside pot and pot lid fits securely.* heatproof plate, metal trivet and rice cooker *If you don't have a trivet, use an empty tuna-type can with both ends removed. Make sure plate fits inside rice cooker.*
strawberry huller	pointed end of bottle/can opener
timbale	cookie cutter OR custard cup OR ramekin OR coffee cup
toaster	waffle iron or sandwich maker *Cook buttered bread in waffle iron or sandwich maker until golden brown.* OR oven *Place sliced bread directly on oven rack in a 350° oven and bake until browned as desired.*

If You Don't Have	Use
toothpick *for testing doneness*	uncooked strand of spaghetti OR small wooden skewer OR paring knife
trivet	empty tuna-type can
turkey lifter	kitchen string *Secure kitchen string around turkey before roasting.* *Make handles for lifting.* OR cheesecloth *Place a few large pieces of cheesecloth in roasting pan* *under turkey. Make sure cheesecloth drapes enough to* *use to transfer turkey to a carving board after roasting.*
vegetable slicer	vegetable peeler *Use peeler to create thin slices of vegetables.*
whisk	beater from electric mixer OR egg beater OR 2 forks
yogurt drainer	paper coffee filter in a mesh strainer *Suspend strainer over a bowl to catch liquid.*

This section is designed for cooks who want quick access to helpful cooking information. For example:

ᐟ You want to make a recipe that calls for an exotic form of produce, but don't know what it looks like.

ᐟ You want to cook meat, poultry or fish using an original recipe and need a quick reference for how to proceed.

ᐟ You want a speedy reminder of how to cook grains or dried beans.

ᐟ You want to make candy, but don't have a candy thermometer.

ᐟ You are looking for common volume measurements, recipe equivalents and metric conversions, but don't want to spend time calculating numbers.

All these issues are addressed in this section. Use it as a companion during recipe preparation.

Fresh Produce

The produce found in supermarkets is flown in from all over the world, so many fruits and vegetables are available to consumers all year long. However, most fruits and vegetables have a peak season when they are most flavorful, most plentiful and least expensive. For the best possible quality and flavor, purchase produce that is grown as close to your local area as possible. Following are some general buying guidelines. But don't forget: Always look at, smell and touch the fruits and vegetables you are purchasing to determine if they are right for your needs. If possible, ask your produce clerk to let you taste a sample of the produce before you buy.

apples
The color differs according to variety, but always choose firm, unblemished fruit with no bruising or soft spots.
Best time to buy: fall and winter

apricots
Select slightly firm, unblemished fruit with no bruising.
Best time to buy: May-August

artichokes
Choose firm heads that are heavy for their size. Look for deep green leaves, but slight purple discolorations don't affect the quality.
Best time to buy: March-May

arugula
Look for small leaves with a bright green color. Arugula spoils rapidly, so avoid leaves that are yellowing or appear old. Leaves can vary in shape from almost oval to highly serrated.
Best time to buy: all year

asparagus
Contrary to popular belief, the size of the stalks doesn't affect their tenderness. Buy crisp spears with the buds still closed.
Best time to buy: early spring-summer

avocados
Look for unblemished fruit. Avocados ripen only after being picked. Plan ahead and store unripe avocados in a cool dark place until they reach desired ripeness. For guacamole or other dips, avocados should be very ripe; for sandwiches or salads, avocados should be slightly firm, but will give slightly to light pressure.
Best time to buy: late spring-summer

bananas

Bananas will ripen during storage, so know how quickly you will consume them. Green bananas will last the longest, while bananas that are turning black will last only a brief amount of time. Choose unblemished fruit with no signs of mushiness.

Best time to buy: all year

beans, green

Select crisp, firm beans with no spots or bruises.

Best time to buy: July-September

beans, shell (fava, lima, cranberry)

Look for crisp pods with good-sized beans inside.

Best time to buy: late summer-early fall

beets

The smaller the beet, the sweeter its flavor will be. Look for smooth, unblemished skin. Beet greens should be crisp and fresh-looking.

Best time to buy: June-October

berries, blackberries

Select dark, plump berries with no signs of mushiness or mold.

Best time to buy: June-August

berries, blueberries

Choose blueberries that are uniform in size and have a purplish-blue color. A silvery cast is desirable.

Best time to buy: summer-fall

berries, boysenberries

See blackberries.

Best time to buy: summer

berries, huckleberries

See blueberries. Huckleberries are smaller and darker in color than blueberries and have thicker skin.

Best time to buy: summer

berries, raspberries

Choose firm, plump berries with no signs of excessive moisture or mold. Color should be good for the variety, ranging from golden, to bright red, to purple-black. Stained baskets could indicate poor quality.

Best time to buy: May-November, depending on region

berries, strawberries

Buy fragrant, evenly shaped fruit with no signs of mushiness or wrinkling. Look for a good red color; avoid berries with white patches.

Best time to buy: April-June

bok choy
Purchase bok choy with crisp, bright green leaves and white stalks. Baby bok choy can be used raw or cooked whole. Mature bok choy should be trimmed and sliced. Avoid heads that are wilting or have brown spots.
Best time to buy: all year

broccoli
Look for tight heads. Avoid heads with yellow spots or bruising and thick, woody stalks. Look for an even green color with a purplish cast.
Best time to buy: October-April

Brussels sprouts
Purchase tight, small heads for the most delicate flavor. The color should be bright green and the weight should feel heavy for the size.
Best time to buy: August-March

cabbage, green and red
Choose firm, crisp heads with a fresh smell and no blemishes. Heads should feel heavy for their size.
Best time to buy: all year

cardoons
Purchase firm, celery-sized stalks with a frosty green color.
Best time to buy: winter-spring

carrots
Pick firm carrots with a bright orange color and no cracks in the flesh. Smaller carrots tend to be sweeter. If tops are attached, look for freshness and a bright green color. Remove tops for storage.
Best time to buy: all year

cauliflower
Look for tightly packed heads with a creamy white color. Avoid florets that are yellowing or have brown speckles. If leaves are attached, they should be bright green in color.
Best time to buy: late fall-spring

celery
Buy crisp, smooth stalks that are heavy for their size. Avoid limp or browning stalks and leaves.
Best time to buy: all year

celery root (celeriac)
Select small, firm roots. Smoother roots will be easier to peel. Avoid roots that feel spongy or light.
Best time to buy: September-May

chard, Swiss
Buy chard with crisp, bright green leaves and firm stalks. Stalks can be red or white.
Best time to buy: summer-fall

chayote (mirliton)
Look for a good green color and firm, slightly ridged, bumpy skin. Chayotes resemble avocados in shape.
Best time to buy: October-March

cherries
Look for firm, brightly colored fruit. Wash cherries and remove stems just before using.
Best time to buy: late spring-summer

chicory
Select crisp heads with bright green, ruffled leaves.
Best time to buy: all year

citrus fruits
Look for plump, fragrant fruits with thin skins. The color should be even and typical for the type, but a green cast doesn't necessarily mean poor quality. Many citrus fruits are colored to mask imperfections. Fruits should seem heavy for their size.
Best time to buy: December-March

collard greens
Look for crisp, nicely colored leaves. Avoid bunches with thick, tough ribs and veins.
Best time to buy: winter

corn
Choose tightly husked, fragrant ears with no signs mushiness. Cornsilk should be white or yellow with little dirt and no signs of insect infestation. Avoid shucking until right before using. Ideally, corn should be cooked the same day it is picked; look for it at roadside farmstands during the summer months.
Best time to buy: May-September

cucumbers
Select firm, unblemished cucumbers with no soft spots or shriveling.
Best time to buy: June-September

dandelion greens
Select bright green leaves; the flavor of smaller leaves will be more mellow than larger leaves. Avoid leaves that are yellowing or wilting.
Best time to buy: winter-early spring

eggplant
Purchase smooth, firm eggplant with bright green caps. Skin should be deeply colored and shiny with no bruising or soft spots. Eggplant should feel heavy for its size.
Best time to buy: August-October

endive, Belgian
Look for small, tightly packed heads that are nearly white with pale, yellowish-green tips.
Best time to buy: fall-spring

endive, curly
Select heads with bright green, ruffle-edged leaves. The center of heads will have paler, more tightly packed leaves.
Best time to buy: summer-fall

escarole
Look for bright, medium-green, wavy leaves with no signs of spoiling.
Best time to buy: summer-fall

fennel
Look for crisp, white to light-green bulbs with light-green to medium-green stalks. Bulbs should be relatively clean. The feathery tops should be bright green.
Best time to buy: late fall-spring

figs
Look for good color for the variety, from white, to green, to brown to purple-black. Choose figs that are symmetrical in shape. Figs should yield to slight pressure. Avoid figs that are splitting, mushy or are molding. Figs will ripen during storage.
Best time to buy: summer-fall

garlic
See red, white or yellow onions. Heads should be firm and cloves tightly packed together.
Best time to buy: all year

ginger
Look for smooth, rather than wrinkled, skin. Buy a small amount at a time to ensure freshness.
Best time to buy: all year

grapes
Select firm, but not hard, fruit with no blemishes, bruises or mushiness at the stem end. There will always be a few duds in a bunch. Look for a yellowish-green color for green grapes; burgundy color for red grapes; and deep purple-blue color for purple grapes. Fruit should be securely attached to stems.
Best time to buy: summer-early fall

grapefruit
See citrus

jicama
Look for firm, smooth, unblemished jicama that feels heavy for its size. Smaller jicamas will be less fibrous than large ones.
Best time to buy: November-June

kale

Select small, tender, crisp leaves with a bright color. Avoid heads that are yellowing or wilted.

Best time to buy: December-April

kiwi fruit

Look for slightly soft, unblemished fruit. The softer the kiwi fruit, the sweeter it will be. For slicing, you may want slightly firmer fruit. Kiwi fruit will ripen during storage.

Best time to buy: November-April

kohlrabi

Select small, light-green bulbs with bright green leaves. The bulbs and stems can also be red in color. Avoid bulbs with blemishes, mushiness, or wilting or yellowing leaves.

Best time to buy: spring-fall

kumquat

See citrus

leeks

Pick crisp, clean leeks with the tops still attached. Small to medium-sized leeks have the best flavor. The root end should be white in color; the tops should be bright green with no browning or wilting. Leeks grow in very sandy soil, so don't worry if they appear dirty.

Best time to buy: fall and winter

lemons

See citrus

lettuce

Select heads with crisp leaves and use as soon as possible after purchasing. Avoid heads with droopy, holey or browning leaves, Many varieties go in and out of peak seasons.

Best time to buy: all year; supply goes down and prices go up in winter

limes

See citrus

mangoes

Select smooth, unblemished fruit with yellow and red tones. Mangoes will ripen after purchase. Certain recipes may call for green fruit.

Best time to buy: summer-early fall

melons, cantaloupe

Choose firm, heavy fruit with a fragrant, fruity aroma. Color of rind should be slightly golden; avoid cantaloupes with a green cast.

Best time to buy: June-September

melons, casaba

See cantaloupe

Best time to buy: late summer-early fall

melons, honeydew

Select very heavy, fragrant fruit. When ripe, rind should be creamy white. A pinkish cast also indicates ripeness.
Best time to buy: July-September

melons, watermelon

Look for an even shape. The bright green skin should be dull, rather than shiny. Fruit should feel heavy.
Best time to buy: May-September

mushrooms, brown (cremini)

See white mushrooms; the color will be grayish brown.
Best time to buy: all year

mushrooms, chanterelle

Look for plump, golden-orange mushrooms with a trumpet shape. Caps should be unbroken and the stems should be relatively long and thin.
Best time to buy: summer and winter

mushrooms, cremini

See brown mushrooms

mushrooms, morel

Look for firm, cone-shaped caps with a "brainy" surface. Color should be brown to almost black.
Best time to buy: April-June

mushrooms, porcini (cepe)

Look for a light-brown color. The diameter of caps can vary greatly. Choose large, firm, smooth caps. The underside of caps should be lighter in color than the surface.
Best time to buy: late spring and fall

mushrooms, portobello

Select flat, open caps up to 6 inches in diameter. The "gills" should be entirely showing. Look for a grayish brown color with little dirt clinging to the cap.
Best time to buy: all year

mushrooms, shiitake

Choose plump mushrooms with smooth caps and curled edges. The stems are discarded, so it is not necessary to test for woodiness. The color should be medium brown.
Best time to buy: spring and fall

mushrooms, white

Look for firm, heavy mushrooms with no bruising or soft spots. The caps should tightly enclose the stems, with little or no "gills" showing. Look for small caps and firm stems. The color should be white or off-white.
Best time to buy: all year

mustard greens

Pick small leaves with a rich, dark-green color. Avoid leaves that are wilting or yellowing.
Best time to buy: winter-early spring

nectarines

Select fruit that yields to slight pressure. Avoid fruit with a green cast. Nectarines will ripen during storage.
Best time to buy: late spring-early fall

okra

Pick plump, bright green okra with no bruises. The smaller vegetables are the most tender.
Best time to buy: late summer-early fall

onions, green (scallions)

The bottoms should be white and free of dirt; tops should be bright green and show no signs of wilting. Avoid bunches that are browning.
Best time to buy: all year

onions, red, yellow or white

Look for smooth, hard, dry onions with no soft spots or mushiness. A bluish cast indicates molding. Avoid onions with green offshoots or dark spots.
Best time to buy: all year

onions, sweet (Walla Walla, Maui, Vidalia)

See red, yellow or white onions.
Best time to buy: April-September; season depends on variety

oranges

See citrus

papayas

Papayas are often sold green in the supermarket, but will ripen during storage. Select fruit with smooth, unblemished skin. Papayas will turn yellow and soften as they ripen. Underripe fruit can be used for cooking.
Best time to buy: spring

parsnips

Look for crisp parsnips with smooth skin. For the sweetest and most tender parsnips, buy the smallest ones available.
Best time to buy: October-February

peaches

Buy smooth, fragrant fruit that gives slightly to the touch. Fruit should have a yellow, rather than green, cast. Peaches will ripen during storage.
Best time to buy: May-September

pears

Select smooth fruit with no signs of bruising or mushiness. Browning on the surface is not necessarily a sign of poor quality. Ripe pears will give slightly to light pressure; only buy ripe pears if using immediately. Buy underripe pears if planning to keep for a few days; they will ripen during storage. Different varieties of pears have slightly different textures when ripe.

Best time to buy: late summer-winter

peas, English

Purchase small, crisp pods, but feel pods to be sure there are peas inside. Large peas will be mealy in texture, but can be used for purees.

Best time to buy: spring-early summer

peas, snow and sugar snap

Look for small, crisp unblemished pods with a bright green color.

Best time to buy: late winter-early summer

peppers, bell

Select firm, heavy, unblemished peppers. Skin should be free of wrinkles. Color should be true to the type and bright. Evenly shaped bell peppers are easier to use in recipes than odd-shaped ones.

Best time to buy: summer-fall

peppers, chile

Look for well-shaped chiles with crisp flesh and a bright, shiny color that is typical for the type. The skin should be smooth and free of cracks or blemishes. The stem ends should show no signs of mold.

Best time to buy: July-October

pineapple

Select fruits that give slightly to the touch, with bright, crisp leaves. The rind will vary in color. Fruit should smell sweet, not sour. Avoid those with wet bottoms or rotting patches.

Best time to buy: March-July

plantains

Look for green or brown fruit, depending on intended use. Dark-brown plantains will be slightly sweet, like a banana. Bright green plantains will taste more like a cooked potato.

Best time to buy: all year

plums

Select slightly firm, smooth, unblemished fruit with no bruises or mushiness. Color should be good for the variety. Plums will ripen during storage.

Best time to buy: May-September

pomelos

See citrus

potatoes
Pick smooth, firm potatoes; avoid those with soft spots, sprouts or tinges of green.
Best time to buy: all year

potatoes, sweet
See potatoes. Look for well-shaped sweet potatoes with either thin, light-brown skin, or thick, dark brown skin, depending on the type.
Best time to buy: all year

pumpkins
Pick small pumpkins for the sweetest flavor. Pumpkins should be heavy for their size, have no visible cracks and have few blemishes.
Best time to buy: fall-winter

radishes
Look for smooth, firm radishes with crisp greens. Avoid greens that a slimy or browning.
Best time to buy: all year

rhubarb
Select slender, crisp stalks with crisp leaves, if still attached. Discard leaves, as they are poisonous. Color should be bright red or light pink, depending on the type.
Best time to buy: April-June

rutabagas
Purchase smooth, firm rutabagas with no cracks. Smaller rutabagas are more tender than large ones.
Best time to buy: October-March

scallions
See green onions

shallots
See red, yellow or white onions
Best time to buy: all year

spinach
Select dark green, crisp leaves with no signs of wilting or yellowing.
Best time to buy: all year

squash, acorn
See winter squash

squash, butternut
See winter squash

squash, pattypan
See summer squash

squash, spaghetti

Choose squash that feels heavy for its size. The color of the thick shell should be light yellow; avoid those with a greenish cast. Avoid squash with soft spots or molding.

Best time to buy: late summer-winter

squash, summer (pattypan, yellow crookneck, zucchini)

Look for small, smooth, firm squash. The color should be good for the type and the skin slightly shiny.

Best time to buy: spring-summer

squash, winter (acorn, butternut)

Buy hard squash that feels heavy for its size. The skin should be relatively smooth with no blemishes.

Best time to buy: September-March

squash, yellow crookneck

See summer squash

squash, zucchini

See summer squash

tangerines

See citrus

tomatillos

Select firm, compact, light green fruit wrapped in brown, papery husks. Husks should be dry and fit tightly around the fruit.

Best time to buy: all year

tomatoes

Select bright, somewhat firm, unblemished fruit. The color should be good for the type. Avoid tomatoes with green or white patches. Try to find "vine-ripened" varieties, but tomatoes will ripen during storage. Do not refrigerate tomatoes or the texture will become mealy. Overripe tomatoes can be cooked into a sauce.

Best time to buy: June-October

turnips

Choose small, smooth, firm turnips with no bruising or discoloration. Tops, if attached, should be bright green and unwilted.

Best time to buy: late spring and early fall

watercress

Choose bright green, crisp leaves with no signs of yellowing or wilting.

Best time to buy: all year

zucchini

See summer squash

Roasting Meats

The ideal way to determine the degree of doneness when roasting meats is to measure the internal temperature. For best results, read the following tips and use the chart below as a guideline.

- Measure your oven's temperature with an oven thermometer to ensure proper calibration.
- Use an instant-read thermometer to measure the internal temperature of the meat. Insert the thermometer into the thickest part of the meat and avoid touching any bones.
- The temperature of the meat will rise from 5° to 10° after being removed from the oven. You may wish to remove the meat from the oven before it reaches the final temperature.
- Let large pieces of meat rest for 15 minutes prior to carving. The juices will redistribute throughout the meat.
- Many factors can affect the timing of roasting meats, such as the meat's size and shape, as well as slight variations in your oven's heat.
- Meats with bones conduct heat better and cook faster than meats without bones. Stuffed meats cook more slowly.

	Rare*	Medium*	Well-Done
Beef	125°-130°	140°	160°
Lamb	130°	150°	170°
Pork	—	—	160°
Veal	—	—	160°

Some health authorities discourage eating undercooked meat due to possible bacterial contamination.

Roasting Poultry

The ideal way to test roasted poultry for doneness is to measure its internal temperature. For best results, read the following guidelines. All poultry should be roasted to a minimum internal temperature of 165°.

- Measure your oven's temperature with an oven thermometer to ensure proper calibration.

- Use an instant-read thermometer to measure the internal temperature of the poultry. Insert the thermometer into the thickest part of the thigh, close to the body, without touching any bones.

- The temperature of large birds will rise from 5° to 10° after being removed from the oven. You may wish to remove the poultry from the oven before it reaches the final temperature.

- Let poultry rest for 10 to 15 minutes prior to carving. The juices will redistribute throughout the bird.

- For small whole chickens, or other birds under 6 pounds, estimate 20 to 25 minutes per pound of roasting time in a 350° oven.

- For large whole chickens, or other birds over 6 pounds, estimate 12 to 15 minutes per pound of roasting time in a 350° oven. The larger the bird, the less roasting time it will need per pound.

- Stuffed poultry will roast more slowly than unstuffed poultry; add about 10 minutes per pound to the cooking time.

- Many factors can affect the timing of roasting poultry, such as the poultry's size and shape, as well as slight variations in your oven's heat.

Cooking Fish

The cooking time for fish depends on many things, such as the type of flesh, the type of cut, the freshness of the fish and other factors. Following is a general rule for estimating fish's cooking time.

- Measure the thickness of the fish at its thickest point.
- Cook fish for about 10 minutes per inch at the thickest point.

Cooking Grains

In a heavy saucepan, bring water, stock or other liquid to a boil. Add grain and stir briefly. Reduce heat to low, cover tightly and simmer until done. Let cooked grains stand uncovered for about 5 minutes and fluff grains with a fork.

NOTE: *If some liquid remains in the pan after the grain is fully cooked, drain liquid.*

Grain	Liquid-to-Grain Ratio	Cooking Time
barley, whole	3:1	1 hour
bulgur wheat	2:1	15-20 minutes
cornmeal	2:1	30 minutes; stir frequently
couscous, instant	1:1	None; let stand for 5 minutes
hominy, whole	2:1	$2\frac{1}{2}$-3 hours
hominy grits	3:1	15-25 minutes
kasha	2:1	15-20 minutes
millet	$2\frac{1}{2}$:1	30-40 minutes
oats, old-fashioned	1-2:1	5-10 minutes; stir frequently
polenta	2-3:1	15-20 minutes; stir frequently
quinoa	2:1	12-17 minutes
rice, aromatic	2:1	15-20 minutes
rice, brown	2:1	40-50 minutes
rice, long-grain white	2:1	20-25 minutes
rice, wild	$3\frac{1}{2}$-4:1	45-60 minutes

Cooking Dried Beans

Most dried beans need to be soaked before cooking. Place beans in a large container and cover with 3 to 4 times as much water as beans. The beans will expand quite a bit, so make sure the container is large enough to accommodate them. Cover container and place in the refrigerator overnight. Discard the soaking water and use fresh, cold water for cooking.

If you don't have time to soak beans overnight, use the quick-soaking method. Place beans in a saucepan and cover with water. Bring to a boil and boil for 2 minutes. Remove pan from heat, cover and let stand for 1 to 2 hours. Drain and cook beans with fresh, cold water.

To cook, bring soaked beans and a large amount of water to a boil in a large saucepan. Reduce heat to low and gently simmer beans until done. You may need to add a little more water while the beans are cooking. Do not add salt to the beans until they are almost done or it could toughen them.

Type	Soak?	Cooking Time
black (turtle)	yes	$1\frac{1}{2}$ hours
black-eyed peas	no	$1\frac{1}{2}$ hours
butter	yes	$1\frac{1}{2}$-2 hours
cranberry	yes	1-$1\frac{1}{4}$ hours
fava	yes	$2\frac{1}{2}$-3 hours
garbanzo (chickpeas)	yes	2-3 hours
great Northern	yes	1-$1\frac{1}{2}$ hours
kidney	yes	$1\frac{1}{2}$-2 hours
lentils	no	35-45 minutes
marrow	yes	1-$1\frac{3}{4}$ hours
lima	yes	$1\frac{1}{2}$-2 hours
navy	yes	$1\frac{1}{2}$-2 hours
pea	yes	45-60 minutes
pink	yes	1-$1\frac{1}{2}$ hours
pinto	yes	$1\frac{1}{2}$-2 hours
red	yes	$\frac{1}{2}$-2 hours
split peas	no	30-45 minutes

Candy-Making Temperatures

Many candy recipes require taking a reading of temperatures, usually of water-sugar syrups. If you don't have a candy thermometer, drop a little of the syrup into ice-cold water; the consistency of the syrup will give you an idea of its temperature.

thread stage
230°-234°
Syrup forms a thin, but soft, thread when dropped into cold water.

soft ball stage
234°-240°
Syrup forms a ball when dropped into cold water; ball flattens when picked up with fingers.

firm ball stage
244°-248°
Syrup forms a ball when dropped into cold water; ball flattens with slight pressure.

hard ball stage
250°-266°
Syrup forms a ball when dropped into cold water; ball is only slightly pliable.

soft crack stage
270°-290°
Syrup forms bendable threads when dropped into cold water.

hard crack stage
300°-310°
Syrup forms hard, brittle threads when dropped into cold water.

caramel stage
310°-338°
Caramelization occurs; syrup turns brown.

Recipe Equivalents and Pan Volumes

Common Recipe Equivalents

Use this chart to easily convert common volume measurements in recipes.

dash	=	$\frac{1}{16}$-$\frac{1}{8}$ tsp.		
pinch	=	less than $\frac{1}{8}$ tsp.		
3 tsp.	=	1 tbs.	=	$\frac{1}{2}$ fluid oz.
2 tbs.	=	$\frac{1}{8}$ cup	=	1 fluid oz.
4 tbs.	=	$\frac{1}{4}$ cup	=	2 fluid oz.
$5\frac{1}{3}$ tbs.	=	$\frac{1}{3}$ cup	=	about 3 fluid oz.
8 tbs.	=	$\frac{1}{2}$ cup	=	4 fluid oz. (1 gill)
$10\frac{2}{3}$ tbs.	=	$\frac{2}{3}$ cup	=	about 5 fluid oz.
12 tbs.	=	$\frac{3}{4}$ cup	=	6 fluid oz.
16 tbs.	=	1 cup	=	8 fluid oz. ($\frac{1}{2}$ pt.)
2 cups	=	1 pt.	=	16 fluid oz.
4 cups	=	1 qt.	=	32 fluid oz.
4 quarts	=	1 gal.	=	140 fluid oz.

Common Pan Volumes

The best way to measure the volume of a pan is to fill it with water and transfer the water to a measuring cup. However, here are some approximate guidelines.

11 x 7	=	2 qt.	=	8 cups
10 x 6	=	$1\frac{1}{2}$ qt.	=	6 cups
9 x 13	=	3 qt.	=	12 cups
9 x 9	=	$1\frac{3}{4}$ qt.	=	7 cups
9-inch round	=	$1\frac{1}{2}$ qt.	=	6 cups
8 x 8	=	$1\frac{1}{2}$ qt.	=	6 cups
8-inch round	=	$1\frac{1}{4}$ qt.	=	5 cups
standard muffin	=	$\frac{1}{4}$-$\frac{1}{2}$ cup	=	4-8 tbs.
mini muffin	=	$\frac{1}{8}$-$\frac{1}{4}$ cup	=	2-4 tbs.

Metric Equivalents

Many recipes from other parts of the world measure ingredients in metric units. This chart will help convert recipes from metric to standard US measurements. The numbers in the chart have been slightly rounded.

Volume

1 tbs.	=	½ fluid oz.	=	14.8 ml.
2 tbs.	=	1 fluid oz.	=	29.5 ml.
¼ cup	=	2 fluid oz.	=	59.1 ml.
½ cup	=	4 fluid oz.	=	118.3 ml.
1 cup	=	8 fluid oz.	=	237 ml.
2 cups	=	16 fluid oz.	=	473 ml.
4 cups	=	32 fluid oz.	=	946 ml.
4 qt.	=	1 gal.	=	3.75 l.

- To convert measurements from milliliters to fluid ounces, divide the measurement in milliliters by 29.57

- To convert measurements from fluid ounces to milliliters, multiply the measurement in ounces by 29.57

Weight

1 oz.	=	30 g.		
4 oz.	=	¼ lb.	=	125 g.
8 oz.	=	½ lb.	=	250 g.
16 oz.	=	1 lb.	=	500 g.
32 oz.	=	2 lb.	=	1 kg.

- To convert measurements from grams to ounces, divide the measurement in grams by 28.35

- To convert measurements from ounces to grams, multiply the measurement in ounces by 28.35

acidulated water: Water treated with a small amount of acid, such as vinegar or citrus juice. It is used to keep vegetables, such as artichokes, CARDOONS and CELERY ROOT, from turning brown after being exposed to air.

aioli: A Mediterranean-style garlic-flavored mayonnaise. It is often used as a dipping sauce.

all-purpose flour: A mixture of hard wheat and soft wheat flours used to make many common baked goods.

allspice: The berry of a tree native to Jamaica. It is sometimes mistakenly thought of as a combination of spices, such as cinnamon, nutmeg and cloves. Whole allspice looks like a small peppercorn.

almond paste: Mainly a mixture of ground almonds, sugar and almond extract, almond paste is used as a filling in pastries, candies and cakes. It is also the main ingredient in marzipan.

applejack: Wood-aged American apple brandy.

apple juice concentrate: A concentrate that makes apple juice when mixed with water. It can be found in cans in the supermarket's freezer case. For cooking, it is usually used undiluted.

Arborio rice: An Italian rice strain with short, fat grains and a high starch content. Arborio rice is the classic choice for making risotto.

arugula: A peppery salad green. It is also called rocket or roquette.

Asiago cheese: Usually sold in this country as a hard grating cheese, it can be found in Italy in many different forms. Asiago's mild, nutty flavor comes from cow's milk.

armagnac: An aged brandy made near the Bordeaux region of France.

basmati rice: An aromatic long-grain rice from India with a distinctive, perfumed aroma. Look for it in gourmet stores, Indian markets or the specialty food aisle of your supermarket.

Belgian endive: Bitter greens used for salads or for cooking. The squat, torpedo-shaped heads are grown in the dark to achieve a pale green, almost white color.

bok choy: A member of the cabbage family, bok choy is a common ingredient in Chinese cookery. It is also called Chinese white cabbage.

beurre manie: A paste made of softened butter and flour that is used for thickening. Literally, the name means "kneaded butter."

blackening spices: A mixture of flavorful spices that is rubbed over a piece of meat, poultry or fish before searing over very high heat. The cooking method forms a black crust that seals in the juices of the food. Blackening spices are commonly used in New Orleans-style cuisine.

bouquet garni: An herb bundle used to flavor soups, stocks and sauces. The classic French formula consists of thyme, parsley and bay leaves, but cooks often add other ingredients, such as celery, leeks, carrots, fennel or other herbs, to customize their dishes. The bouquet garni should be removed from the dish before serving.

bread flour: A high-gluten wheat flour used to make yeast breads.

Brie cheese: This soft cow's milk cheese has an edible white rind. The interior is the color of butter and becomes slightly runny when perfectly ripe and warmed to room temperature.

brown mushrooms: Also called cremini mushrooms, these look like white mushrooms with a medium-brown color. Their flavor is a little deeper and earthier than white mushrooms.

bulgur wheat: A staple in Middle Eastern cooking, bulgur is processed whole wheat. It is often used to make pilafs, stuffings and salads, such as tabbouleh.

Cajun spice blend: A bold mixture of spices for seasoning Cajun-style dishes, such as jambalaya. Each cook and manufacturer has his/her own special formula.

cake flour: A soft wheat flour with a high starch content that is used to make delicate cakes or pastries. It can also be called pastry flour.

Calvados: An apple brandy made in the Normandy region of France.

Camembert cheese: Similar to BRIE, Camembert is named for the French town of its origin.

candied ginger: Also called crystallized ginger, this is sliced or chopped fresh ginger that has been simmered in a sugar-water solution, coated with additional sugar and dried.

capon: A castrated young rooster raised especially for eating.

cardamom: A potent spice, which is native to India. Its pods contain many seeds and both the pods and the seeds can be used for cooking. In addition to Indian cuisine, it is also popular in Scandinavian cooking.

carob: This chocolate substitute comes from the pods of a tropical tree.

capers: The small flower buds of the caper bush, which is native to the Mediterranean. These buds are pickled in salty brine and used to flavor many traditional French, Italian and Spanish dishes. For the best flavor, rinse capers before using to remove excess salt from the surface.

cardoons: A vegetable that resembles celery, but tastes like an artichoke. Like artichokes, cardoons should be placed into ACIDULATED WATER after cutting to prevent browning.

celery root (celeriac): This gnarled, brown root tastes somewhat like celery. Celery root must be peeled before using and should be placed into ACIDULATED WATER to keep it from turning brown. It can be eaten raw or cooked.

chantrelle mushrooms: These wild mushrooms have an unexpected yellow color and trumpet-like shape. Their flavor is delicate, earthy and nutty.

chayote (mirliton): A type of squash resembling a green avocado. Its flavor is like summer squash, but its texture is more crisp.

chèvre: Chèvre, the French word for goat, refers to any cheese made from the milk of goats. The texture of these cheeses can differ greatly, but the most common form of chèvre on the US market comes in soft, moist logs.

chervil: A fragile herb from the parsley family, chervil is one of the main ingredients in FINES HERBES. Its leaves are small, feathery and medium green in color. Since its flavor is so delicate, it is best to add chervil to dishes at the end of the cooking time, or to dishes that will not withstand high heat.

chicory: A bitter green that can be used in salad mixtures or cooked. It it often confused with CURLY ENDIVE.

chile powder: This powder is made from only ground chile peppers. It can be confused with chili powder, in which other ground spices are blended with the ground chiles.

Chinese chile oil: A chile pepper-infused oil used to add flavor and heat to Chinese dishes.

Chinese five-spice powder: A powerful mixture of cinnamon, cloves, fennel seeds, star anise and SZECHWAN PEPPERCORNS used to flavor Chinese dishes.

citrus stripper: A tool for removing wide strips of citrus peel. It is useful when making "twists" of lemon or lime for cocktails or espresso drinks.

citrus zester: A tool for removing just the colored part of citrus peels, which is called the ZEST. When the tool is dragged across the surface of the fruit, threads of citrus zest are formed. Tip: before zesting, wash the citrus fruit well with soap and water to remove any trace of wax or pesticide.

clarified butter: Also called ghee, clarified butter is the golden liquid left over after slowly melting butter and separating it from its milk solids. Clarified butter can withstand high cooking temperatures because there are no milk solids left to burn. It also keeps for long periods of time without spoiling.

cognac: A special type of brandy named after the town in western France where it is made. Cognac can be purchased at different stages of aging.

Cointreau: A clear, orange-flavored liqueur from France.

coulis: A French term referring to a thick, uncooked puree or sauce. A coulis can be made from vegetables or fruits, such as tomatoes, red bell peppers, corn, berries, mangoes and other items.

court-bouillon: A highly flavored broth used for poaching foods, such as fish.

couscous: Small round grains of pasta, which are common in North African cooking. Couscous can be used for pilafs, salads, side dishes and as a base for vegetarian entrées.

crab boil: A mixture of herbs and spices used to season boiled crab, shrimp or other shellfish.

cranberry beans: Fresh cranberry beans grow in large shells that are speckled with red. The beans themselves are off-white with the same red markings. The red color turns to brownish red in the dried form.

crème anglaise: A rich vanilla-flavored custard sauce.

crème chantilly: Whipped cream flavored with a small amount of sugar and vanilla extract or liqueur.

crème fraiche: Literally "fresh cream," crème fraiche is actually a cultured, thickened cream, similar to diluted sour cream. The flavor is rich and tangy and the texture is like yogurt.

cremini mushrooms: See brown mushrooms.

Creole seasoning: A potent mixture of spices for seasoning Creole-style dishes, such as gumbo. Each cook and manufacturer has his or her own special formula.

Curaçao: An orange-flavored liqueur from the Caribbean.

curly endive: This bitter green grows in loose heads of curly leaves. It can be used raw in salads or cooked. It is sometimes mistaken for CHICORY.

daikon radish: A large white radish, also called a Japanese radish. The texture and flavor is similar to a radish, but it's not quite as as spicy.

dandelion greens: Bitter greens that can be eaten raw in salads or cooked. Smaller, younger leaves are best for salads; larger, older leaves are best for cooking.

dry Jack cheese: A variation of Monterey Jack cheese that has been aged until it is dry and hard, like Parmesan. The flavor transforms from mild and creamy to tangy and slightly sharp through the aging process.

dry rubs: Also called dry marinades, these are mixtures of herbs, spices and other flavorings that are rubbed onto meat, poultry or fish before cooking.

Edam cheese: A cow's milk cheese from Holland that can be recognized by its shiny red wax coating. The cheese itself is slightly yellow and it has a distinctive, nutty flavor.

egg substitute: A liquid egg product in which the egg yolks are replaced with oil, milk powder and other ingredients. Use it as you would any beaten eggs. It can be found in the refrigerator or freezer case of the supermarket.

Emmentaller cheese: A version of Swiss cheese from the Emmental valley in Switzerland.

endive: see BELGIAN ENDIVE; CURLY ENDIVE

escarole: A bitter green that can be used raw in salads or cooked. Its flavor is a little milder than CURLY ENDIVE.

farmer's cheese: A moist, firm, cow's milk cheese. The flavor is fresh and slightly tangy.

fava beans: These beans can be found fresh, in their shells, or dried. Fava beans resemble large lima beans in appearance, but their flavor is somewhat different. Fresh favas must be first shelled, then blanched, which helps to remove the tough skin around the beans. Fava beans are popular ingredients in Middle Eastern and Mediterranean cuisines.

fennel fronds: The feathery green tops of fennel bulbs, which can be chopped and used as an anise-flavored herb.

fenugreek: One of the primary flavors in Indian curry powder, fenugreek seeds have a distinctive sweet-sour aroma and flavor. Fenugreek originates in Asia and southern Europe. Look for the seeds in specialty food stores and health food stores.

feta cheese: In the US, much of the feta cheese on the market is made from cow's milk. However, in its native Greece, feta is made with sheep's or goat's milk. The flavor of feta is salty and tangy; sheep's or goat's milk feta is even tangier. Feta has a crumbly texture and can often be found packed in its own brine.

fines herbes: A traditional French mixture of chopped fresh or dried parsley, tarragon, chives and chervil. Fresh herbs should be added to the dish toward the end of cooking time to prevent flavor loss; dried herbs should be added toward the beginning of cooking time to give their flavors a chance to develop.

focaccia: An Italian flatbread flavored variously with olive oil, coarse salt, fresh herbs, onions or other items.

frisee: A bitter salad green with very curly, light green to white leaves.

galangal: Similar to ginger, this root-like vegetable is used in Southeast Asian cooking.

ganache: A rich mixture of chocolate, cream and flavorings that is used as a dessert glaze or filling.

garam masala: Literally "warm mixture," garam masala is a general term for a spice blend common in India. Each cook has his or her own special combination of spices.

Gorgonzola cheese: A pungent, aged, blue cheese from Italy. It is made with cow's milk.

Gouda cheese: Similar to EDAM, Gouda is another Holland export. This cow's milk cheese has a mild nutty flavor and smooth, creamy texture. The rind may still have a portion of the yellow wax covering that surrounds the wheels before they are cut into pieces for purchase.

graham flour: Coarsely ground whole wheat flour. It is also an old-fashioned term for WHOLE WHEAT FLOUR.

Grand Marnier: An orange-flavored liqueur from France.

great Northern beans: These white beans resemble a large lima bean in shape. They are most often available dried.

grenadine: A sweet, dark-red syrup, originally made from pomegranates. It is used to flavor marinades, beverages and desserts.

Gruyère cheese: Hailing from its namesake village in Switzerland, Gruyère is a cow's milk cheese with a distinctive nutty flavor. It is the main ingredient in traditional Swiss cheese fondue.

hard sauce: A mixture of butter, sugar and flavorings that is refrigerated until solid. Slices of hard sauce are placed on hot desserts, such as plum pudding, and form a sauce when melted.

haricot vert: Literally "green been" in French, this has come to be known as a special, slender variety of young green beans.

herbes de Provence: A mixture of herbs common in the Provence region of France for seasoning a variety of dishes.

hominy: Large corn kernels that have been processed and treated with a special lime or lye solution.

hominy grits: Ground HOMINY, which can be served as a breakfast cereal or side dish. It is a typical ingredient in the cooking of the southern US.

Jarlsberg cheese: Jarlsberg looks and tastes like Swiss cheese, but comes from Norway.

jasmine rice: An aromatic long-grain rice imported from Thailand with a distinctive, floral aroma. Look for it in the specialty food aisle of the supermarket, gourmet stores or Asian markets.

jelly bag: A special tool used to strain and clarify fruit juices when making jelly.

jicama: This large, round vegetable has a brown, fibrous exterior, which, when peeled, reveals a juicy, crunchy, white interior. It can be eaten raw or cooked.

kasha: Hulled grains of buckwheat, which are often used in Eastern European cooking. Kasha can be used to make pilafs, stuffings and cereals.

kippers: Herring that has been "kippered," or cured through a special process of salting and smoking.

kohlrabi: A vegetable similar to a mild turnip.

kumquat: A very small citrus fruit with an orange-colored peel and tart flesh. It can be eaten raw or cooked, with or without the peel.

ladyfingers: Sponge cake that is shaped to resemble large, flat fingers. Ladyfingers can be used as a base for elegant desserts or to line dessert molds.

lavender: An herb popular in southern French cuisine. Lavender's aroma and flavor is pleasant and soothing. In fact, its scent is rumored to have a relaxing effect. Its gray-green leaves and purple flowers can be used fresh or dried to flavor any type of dish, but they are most frequently used in desserts and teas.

lemon grass: A stalk-like, fibrous herb common in Southeast Asian cuisine. It resembles a pale green onion. Its sour lemon flavor has a gingery punch.

lovage: An herb that resembles celery leaves in appearance and flavor.

mace: The outer covering of the nutmeg seed. Its flavor is a little bit stronger than nutmeg's.

maitre d'hotel butter: A classic French compound butter for accompanying grilled or broiled meats, poultry and seafood.

marjoram: This herb, common in Mediterranean cooking, looks and tastes like a delicate version of OREGANO.

marrow beans: Very large white beans, usually found dried.

Marsala: A fortified wine from Sicily.

mascarpone cheese: A very rich cream cheese from Italy. Mascarpone's velvety texture and rich flavor come from its high butterfat content.

millet: Although we might recognize it as bird seed, this grain is a great addition to pilafs and baked goods.

mirin: A dry rice wine used in Japanese cooking.

monkfish: A large, very ugly fish with a firm texture, reminiscent of lobster meat. Its flavor is rich, sweet and meaty and can be cooked in a number of ways. Only its tail is used for cooking.

monounsaturated fats: The healthiest of all fats, monounsaturated fats are known to reduce cholesterol. Oils high in monounsaturated fat include olive oil, canola oil and peanut oil.

morel mushrooms: These wild mushrooms have a pointed cap with a convoluted surface. Their flavor is deep and earthy. The darker the color of the mushroom, the deeper its flavor will be.

86

mortar and pestle: Traditional implements for crushing or grinding spices, herbs and other foods. The mortar is a small, bowl-shaped container, often with a foot for stability. The pestle is a thick wand with a rounded end, which is used to push the foods into and around the interior of the mortar. Common materials for mortars and pestles are marble, stoneware, porcelain and wood.

mulling spices: A mixture of spices used to flavor hot spiced cider or wine.

mustard greens: Bitter, pungent greens used for cooking.

Napa cabbage: Also called Chinese cabbage, Napa cabbage has large, pale-green, ruffled leaves. Its flavor is mild and it can be used raw or cooked.

navy beans: Small white beans, usually found dried.

neufchatel cheese: Originally, neufchatel was named for its namesake village in the Normandy region of France. In this form it is a fresh white cow's milk cheese, similar to cream cheese. In America, neufchatel is sometimes marketed as a reduced-fat cream cheese.

orange juice concentrate: A concentrate that makes orange juice when mixed with water. It can be found in cans in the freezer case of the supermarket. For cooking, it is usually used undiluted.

oregano: There are two main types of oregano, which, sampled side by side, are quite different. Mexican oregano has a stronger, more pungent flavor than Mediterranean oregano and requires a lighter hand when using. Both types of oregano should be used sparingly, as the flavor will readily permeate dishes.

orzo: A type of pasta the size and shape of a large teardrop.

pancetta: An unsmoked Italian bacon, which is cured with salt and other spices. It usually comes in a fat salami-like roll.

parchment paper: A specially designed paper for cooking. Parchment withstands high cooking temperatures, and items baked on it will not stick to its surface.

parsnips: Sweet, nutty root vegetables that resemble carrots, but have an off-white color.

pastry flour: see CAKE FLOUR

pea beans: Small white beans, famous for being the main ingredient in Boston Baked Beans. They are often confused with NAVY BEANS and are usually found dried rather than fresh.

peppercress: A peppery salad green with small, feathery leaves. It is also called garden cress.

pesto: An uncooked Italian sauce or spread made from crushed basil, garlic, nuts, cheese and olive oil. Some cooks vary the herb to complement the dish they are preparing.

pickling spice: A spice blend used to pickle foods. It can also be used as a seasoning when cooking.

pimientos: A type of sweet red pepper. Pimientos are the basis for paprika.

pink beans: Usually found dried, pink beans look like a pale version of pinto beans. They can be used interchangeably with pinto beans.

phyllo dough: Paper-thin sheets of pastry, which are usually layered with CLARIFIED BUTTER to form crisp, flaky specialties, such as baklava.

plantains: A banana variety popular in Latin American and Caribbean cuisines. Plantains resemble large, firm, green bananas.

polenta: Cornmeal that has been specially prepared for making a classic Italian dish of the same name, similar to American cornmeal mush.

polyunsaturated fats: These fats are rumored to reduce cholesterol in the diet. They are considered much healthier than saturated fats. Oils that contain high amounts of polyunsaturated fat are: safflower oil, sunflower oil, corn oil and soybean oil.

pomelo: A Malaysian citrus fruit similar to a grapefruit.

porcini mushrooms: Pale brown wild mushrooms that come from Italy and France (in France they are called cepes). Very few are grown domestically and they are hard to find fresh. Many cooks find rehydrated dried porcinis an adequate substitute when incorporated into a multi-ingredient dish.

portobello mushrooms: These are BROWN (CREMINI) MUSHROOMS that have been allowed to mature. The texture and flavor is like meat when cooked.

potato flour: Also called potato starch, this thickening agent comes from ground cooked potatoes.

prosciutto: A salt-cured, air-dried ham from Italy.

puff pastry: A rich, butter-filled pastry that puffs high as it bakes due to hundreds of layers of butter and dough. When the butter melts it forms steam, which causes the pastry to rise.

quick breads: Breads leavened with baking soda or baking powder instead of with yeast. Quick breads don't require a lengthy rising period before baking.

queso fresco: A Mexican version of FARMER'S CHEESE with a slightly saltier flavor. Look for it in specialty delicatessens or Latin American markets.

quinoa: A super-nutritious grain that originated in the days of the ancient Incas. The grains are small and globular, similar to COUSCOUS. It can be used as a side dish, salad or base for a vegetarian entrée.

ramekin: A small baking dish that usually holds a single serving.

rèmoulade sauce: A classic French sauce used as an accompaniment to shellfish.

rice paper: A thin, translucent wrapper used in Southeast Asian cooking in the same manner as an egg roll wrapper. It must be soaked in water before using to make it pliable.

rice wine: see MIRIN

Roquefort cheese: A salty, piquant blue cheese made in the French village of Roquefort. Its distinctive flavor comes from sheep's milk and a long aging period in limestone caves.

rose water: A fragrant liquid made from rose petals. It is used to flavor desserts.

rutabagas: These are often confused with turnips because their appearance and flavor is similar. The skin of rutabagas is white or pale yellow.

saffron: An expensive spice that is hand-cultivated from the stigmas of special crocuses. It imbues an orange-yellow color and exotic flavor and fragrance into recipes. Saffron is what makes the rice yellow and fragrant in the traditional Spanish dish, paella.

salt pork: A salt-cured slab of pork, which is most often used as a flavoring.

saturated fats: Linked to heart disease and high cholesterol, saturated fats are the ones to avoid. They usually come from animal sources and in their pure form will be solid at room temperature. A few plant sources of saturated fat are coconut oil, palm oil and palm kernel oil.

self-rising flour: A mixture of flour, salt and leavening.

shiitake mushrooms: These mushrooms resemble BROWN (CREMINI) MUSHROOMS, but have larger, flatter caps. The color is usually tan to medium brown and the flavor is meaty and earthy. Shiitakes are common ingredients in Asian cooking.

simple syrup: A syrup made from sugar and water. It is used when a smooth texture is desired in a sweetened product, such as SORBET. It is also good to keep on hand in the summertime for sweetening cold beverages, such as iced tea.

sorbet: A frozen dessert or palate cleanser, most often fruit-flavored. It is made from sugar, water and pureed fruit or other flavorings.

spaetzle: Small German boiled dumplings made from flour, water, eggs and milk.

squab: A type of pigeon that has been raised to be eaten. Squab is considered a small game bird and has dark, sweet flesh.

Stilton cheese: An English blue cheese made from the same mold that produces ROQUEFORT. Cow's milk is used to make this strong, aged cheese.

summer savory: A strongly flavored, leafy herb from the mint family.

superfine sugar: Finely granulated sugar manufactured to dissolve quickly and create a fine texture in recipes. In England it is called castor sugar.

sweet onions: Onion varieties known for their pronounced sweet flavor. The most famous are Maui, Walla Walla and Vidalia.

Szechwan peppercorns: Very different from black peppercorns, these come from the Szechwan province of China, which is known for its spicy cuisine. Look for Szechwan peppercorns in the Asian foods section of the supermarket, or in an Asian market.

tahini: A paste made from ground sesame sesame seeds that is used in Middle Eastern cooking.

tamari: A thicker, darker version of soy sauce.

tamarind: A very sour fruit, whose pulp is commonly used in Indian, Middle Eastern, Latin American and Caribbean cuisines.

Texmati rice: A hybrid of domestic long-grain rice and BASMATI RICE.

timbale: A mold, similar to a RAMEKIN, but usually with a rounded bottom. The term can also refer to the dish that is placed into the mold, which is then unmolded onto a serving plate.

tomatillos: Tomatillos resemble small green tomatoes, but are actually not related to tomatoes at all. They come wrapped in a brown husk, which should be removed and discarded. Tart and acidic, tomatillos can be used raw or cooked. Look for tomatillos with the specialty produce in the supermarket or in Latin American markets.

treacle: The British term for molasses, treacle is a by-product of the sugar refining process.

Triple Sec: A Mexican-style orange-flavored liqueur.

turmeric: Although the color of this spice is similar to SAFFRON, its flavor is more bitter. It costs quite a bit less than saffron. Turmeric is typically found in Indian recipes and is a major component of Indian curry powder.

vanilla sugar: Granulated sugar that has been flavored with vanilla beans.

venison: The meat of a deer, which is very low in fat and rich in flavor.

vermouth: Fortified, flavored red or white wine. The white, rather than the red, variety is most often used for cooking.

vital gluten: Pure wheat protein that, when added to yeast-leavened baked goods, provides structure. Look for it in health food stores or from mail-order grain suppliers.

wasabi: Also called Japanese horseradish, this potent green paste is used in sushi preparation. It can be found as a paste or powder in Asian markets or the international section of the supermarket.

whole wheat flour: Wheat flour that still contains the wheat germ.

yogurt cheese: Yogurt from which much of the liquid has been drained from the milk solids. Nonfat yogurt cheese can be used as a healthy substitute for cream cheese.

zest: The colored part of citrus peels, which contains volatile, aromatic oils.

Bibliography

2001 Household Hints and Dollar Stretchers. J.G. Ferguson, 1997.

Baking Masters. Http://www.bakingmasters.com. 1997.

Bellerson, Karen J. *The Complete & Up-to-Date Fat Book.* Garden City Park, NY: Avery, 1993.

Bennett, Cleaves M. and Newport, Christine. *Control Your High Blood Pressure Cookbook.* New York: Doubleday, 1987.

Better Homes and Gardens Cookbook. New York: Bantam, 1981.

Child, Julia. *Mastering the Art of French Cooking.* New York: Knopf, 1961.

The Chile Heads' Home Page. Http://neptune.netimages.com~chile. 1995-97.

Clingerman, Polly. *The Kitchen Companion.* Gaithersburg, MD: The American Cooking Guild, 1994.

Columbia/HCA Healthcare Corporation. Http://www.columbia.net. 1997.

The Cook's Thesaurus. Http://www.northcoast.com/~alden.

Corn, Elaine. *Now You're Cooking.* Emeryville, CA: Harlow & Ratner, 1994.

Crocker, Betty. *Betty Crocker's Lowfat, Low Cholesterol Cookbook.* New York: Prentice-Hall, 1991.

The Culinary Connection. Http://www.culinary.com. 1997.

The Culinary Institute of America. *The New Professional Chef, Fifth Edition.* New York: Van Nostrand Reinhold, 1991.

Cunningham, Marion. *The Fannie Farmer Cookbook.* New York: Knopf, 1990.

DeMedici, Lorenza. *The Best of Italy the Beautiful Cookbook.* San Francisco: Harper SF, 1994.

The Detroit News. Http://www.detnews.com. 1998.

Eating Well On-line. Http://www.eatingwell.com.

Eisenberg, Arlene; Eisenberg, Heidi; Eisenberg, Sandee. *The Special Guest Cookbook.* New York: Beauforr Books, 1982.

The Electronic Gourmet Guide. Http://www.foodwine.com. 1997.

Epicurious. Http://www.epicurious.com.

Escoffier, Auguste. *Le Guide Culinaire.* New York: Van Nostrand Reinhold, 1979.

Eskimo North. Http://www.eskimo.com. 1994-96.

Everybody's Seafood. Http://www.srv.net.

Fanucci, Bob. California Culinary Academy, San Francisco, CA.

Fatfree: The Low Fat Vegetarian Archives. Http://www.fatfree.com. 1993-96.

Fine Cooking. Http://www.taunton.com.

Fine Food and Travel. Http://www.finefishing.com. 1996-97.

Florida Trails. Http://www.floridatrails.com. 1996.

Francine's Yummyzine. Http://www.yummyzine.com. 1997.

The Gate. Http://www.sfgate.com. 1997.

Gibons, Barbara. *Light and Spicy.* New York: Harper & Row, 1989.

Gisslen, Wayne. *Professional Cooking.* New York: Wiley, 1989.

Gisslen, Wayne. *Professional Baking.* New York: Wiley, 1985.

Godzilla. Http://godzilla.eecs.berkeley.edu. 1997.

Good Housekeeping. Http://goodhousekeeping.com. 1997.

Gorman, Judy. *Judy Gorman's Vegetable Cookbook.* New York: MJF Books, 1986.

The Gourmet Connection. Http://gourmetconnection.com. 1995.

The Gourmet Gardener. Http://www.metrobbs.com. 1997.

The Gumbo Pages. Http://www.gumbopages.com.

Heloise. *Hints and Help from Heloise.* New York: Bonanza Books, 1981.

Herbst, Sharon Tyler. *The Food Lover's Companion, Second Edition.* New York: Barron's, 1995.

Reader's Digest. *Household Hints and Handy Tips.* Pleasantville, NY: Reader's Digest, 1988.

Howard, Ben. *Make Your Own Mixes and Prepared Foods.* Highland City, FL: Rainbow Books, 1994.

Internet Traveler. Http://www.everybodys.org. 1997.

Joy of Baking. Http://www.joyofbaking.com. 1997.

Karen's Kitchen. Http://jkgann.com.

Leith, Prue. *The Cook's Handbook*. Wilmington, DE: LDAP, 1981.

Lifetime Online. Http://www.lifetimetv.com. 1997.

Mayo Health Oasis. Http://www.mayo.ivi.com. 1995-97.

McGee, Harold. *On Food and Cooking*. New York: Macmillan, 1984.

Midwest Living. Http://www.midwestliving.com. 1997.

New Orleans Metropolitan Convention and Visitor's Bureau. Http://nawlins.com. 1995.

Nutrasweet. Http://www.nutrasweet.com. 1997.

The Oasis. Http://www.produceoasis.com. 1996.`

Ornish, Dean. *Eat More, Weigh Less*. New York: HarperCollins, 1993.

Palazuelos, Susanna. *The Best of Mexico the Beautiful Cookbook*. San Francisco: Harper SF, 1994.

Peck, Paula. *The Art of Fine Baking*. New York: Barnes and Noble, 1961.

Plutt, Mary Jo. *Prevention's Stop Dieting and Lose Weight*. Emmaus, PA: Rodale Press, 1994.

Prevention's Health Ideas. Http://www.healthyideas.com. 1997.

QVC Online Kitchen. Http://www.qvc.com. 1995-97.

Raintree, Diane. *The Household Book of Hints and Tips*. New York: Jonathan David, 1979.

Redbook. Http://www.redbookmag.com. 1997.

Restaurants and Institutions. Http://www.rimag.com. 1997.

Rinzler, Carol Ann. *What to Use Instead*. New York: Pharos Books, 1987.

Rombauer, Irma S. and Becker, Marion Rombauer. *The Joy of Cooking*. New York: Penguin, 1964.

Rosso, Julee and Lukins, Sheila. *The New Basics*. New York: Workman, 1989.

Roth, Harriet. *Harriet Roth's Cholesterol-Control Cookbook*. New York: NAL, 1989.

Salt and Pepper. Http://www.saltandpepper.com. 1997.

Scotto, Marianne; Scotto, Michèle; Scotto, Elisabeth. *The Best of France the Beautiful Cookbook*. San Francisco: Harper SF, 1994.

The Slimming Partner. Http://www.microskills.com. 1997.

The State of Alabama Department of Public Health. Http://www.alapubhealth.org.

Sue's Recipe Server. Http://www.hubcom.com. 1995-97.

Sugarplums. Http://www.sugarplums.com. 1996-97.

Sunset Fresh Produce. Menlo Park, CA: Lane, 1987.

Sunset Good Cook's Handbook. Menlo Park, CA: Lane, 1986.

Sunset Seafood Cookbook. Menlo Park, CA: Lane, 1981.

Sonnenschmidt, Frederick H. and Nicolas, John F. *The Art of Garde Manger*. New York: Van Nostrand Reinhold, 1993.

Tante Marie's Cooking School. Http://www.tantemarie.com. 1997.

Top Secret Recipes. Http://www.topsecretrecipes.com. 1997.

United States Department of Agriculture. Http://www.usda.gov.

University of California Berkeley. Http://server.berkeley.edu. 1997.

University of Illinois, College of Agricultural, Consumer and Environmental Sciences, Horticultue Solutions Series. Http://www.envirolink.org.

University of Pennsylvania School of Art and Sciences. Http://www.sas.upenn.edu. 1997.

Vintages. Http://www.vintages.com.

The Virtual Vegetarian. Http://www.vegetariantimes.com. 1997.